Tracey Cox i̶̶̶̶̶̶ (and hottest) ̶̶̶̶̶̶̶ on sex and relationships, and is also a TV presenter. Her numerous appearances include *Hotter Sex* and the BBC's *Would Like to Meet*. She writes a regular column for the *Sunday Times* Style magazine and *Closer*. Tracey was born in England and spent many years in Australia where she was associate editor of *Cosmopolitan*. She has a degree in psychology, is the web sexpert for handbag.com and contributes regularly to leading women's magazines across the globe. Her books *Hot Sex* and *Hot Relationships* are international bestsellers. She lives in Richmond, London.

Also by Tracey Cox

HOT SEX
HOT SEX POCKET EDITION
HOT RELATIONSHIPS

and published by Corgi Books

HOT LOVE

HOW TO GET IT

POCKET EDITION

TRACEY COX

CORGI BOOKS

HOT LOVE: Pocket Edition
A CORGI BOOK : 0 552 14955 1

First publication in Great Britain

PRINTING HISTORY
Corgi pocket edition published 2003

3 5 7 9 10 8 6 4 2

Set in Galliard, Frutiger and Humanist
by Phoenix Typesetting, Burley-in-Wharfedale, West Yorkshire.

Corgi Books are published by Transworld Publishers,
61–63 Uxbridge Road, London W5 5SA,
a division of The Random House Group Ltd,
in Australia by Random House Australia (Pty) Ltd,
20 Alfred Street, Milsons Point, Sydney, NSW 2061, Australia,
in New Zealand by Random House New Zealand Ltd,
18 Poland Road, Glenfield, Auckland 10, New Zealand
and in South Africa by Random House (Pty) Ltd,
Endulini, 5a Jubilee Road, Parktown 2193, South Africa.

Printed and bound in Great Britain by
Clays Ltd, St Ives plc.

Contents

Introduction ix

1 WOULD LIKE TO MEET . . . 1

2 OK, I THINK I'VE FOUND THEM 65

3 GETTING SERIOUS 101

4 SEX: THE GLUE WHICH STICKS YOU TOGETHER 131

5 SEX TROUBLESHOOTING: THE 8 MOST-ASKED COUPLE QUESTIONS 169

6 AND IF IT ALL GOES HORRIBLY WRONG . . . 187

HOT
LOVE

POCKET EDITION

Introduction
••••••••••••••••••••••••••••••••••

I told my best friend I was writing a book about relationships and she spat wine halfway across the bar.

'You can't!' she said. 'You're, you know, *divorced*!'

'Oh my *God*!' I said. 'I'd completely forgotten.'

Not. Look, I admit it. It doesn't make me feel terribly confident either when I'm described as 'Sex and Relationships Expert. Divorced'. It does sound like a contradiction in terms, so I thought I'd better explain myself up front.

What qualifies me as a relationships 'expert'? Well, I've got a psychology degree. I've also spent more than a decade writing, researching and talking about sex and relationships. I was *Cosmopolitan*'s agony aunt, presented a talkback radio show and lots of telly programmes on relationships as well as website stuff and body language research – oh, and I've had, er, lots of practice. I've been married and divorced. I've had six-week flings, several two-year this-must-be-the-one live-in relationships, first-date fizzles, four-year triumphs (and yes, the odd overnighter as well). But if you want reassurance that I met, married and am currently snuggled up on the couch with Mr Bloody Perfect, you're reading the wrong book. I just happen to know a bit more than the average person about relationships on both an academic and personal basis. (And I have to say, out of the two, I've probably learnt more from experience and talking to real people than I have from those psychological studies, however fascinating they are.)

This book is for singles and couples, men and women, heterosexuals, bisexuals, gays and lesbians. While it's predominantly addressed to straight couples (simply because constantly writing girl, boy or boy, boy or girl, girl all the time would have been confusing), all the advice applies to every couple combination.

Unfortunately, reading the book's the easy bit. You could devour *Hot Love* cover to cover, be able to recite extracts off by heart, and still not benefit one iota. Knowledge will only get you so far: you've got to practise what I've preached. That's what people mean when they say, 'You have to work hard at relationships.' You do. But it's not really work, is it? It's more about finding out about each other, exploring each other's minds, hearts and bodies, treating each other nicely and loving each other to death. If that's hard work, I'm volunteering for community service at whatever male model agency Calvin Klein use.

Hot Love will never be finished to my satisfaction because, every day, I discover something new about relationships. The temptation to keep on adding bits is enormous but I had to stop somewhere. So this is it: a selection of the good bits from *Hot Relationships*, packaged into a pocket-size so you can have Hot Love wherever you fancy. Enjoy!

Would Like to Meet . . .

● ●

While this book unashamedly celebrates love, you haven't got a hope of finding a fab partner until you relax about it. Fall in love with being single and all sorts of doors spring open. Of all the single people I know, it's the people who *like* being single, who *aren't* waiting around for their matching bookend, who get asked out the most. They're not gorgeous, just interesting, fun people to be around. So keep reading at your own risk. If my advice works, you might not just end up being happy solo, you might prefer it (at least for a little while). Besides, you've got no *choice* but to enjoy being single. Moon around, focus on all the bad things about it, put everything on hold until 'they' come along and I guarantee you'll be miserable *for life*. You won't be happy single and you won't be happy in a relationship either because – sorry! – you're never going to attract anyone worth knowing with an attitude like that.

Instead of slipping into that woe-is-me stuff, why not rejoice in the freedom and excitement of your current state. After all, you already have a brilliant life-long partner and playmate permanently by your side. You!

Here are 10 more very good reasons why you should jealously guard your singleton status rather than rush into the wrong relationship just for the sake of it . . .

TEN GREAT THINGS ABOUT BEING SINGLE
For him

1. You don't have to answer to *anyone*.

2. No-one rolls their eyes when the remote accidentally sticks on the sports channel.

3. You can clip your toenails without someone vomiting in the background.

4. *Playboy* gets pride of place on the coffee table – and no-one lectures you about how much porn degrades women.

5. You can dress up in your old football shirt and criticize the hell out of the players without someone saying, 'You're kidding yourself. With that beer gut you'd be flat out catching the ball, so don't give him a hard time!'

6. You don't have to tell her she doesn't look fat/her bottom's not big/more than a ➤

handful's a waste.

7. You can masturbate in the middle of the lounge room without fear of her walking in and saying, 'Ohmigod! This must mean you don't want to have sex with *me*.'

8. You can put tomato sauce on *everything* without 'tut-tut's and 'Honestly, Harry, you're such a pig with food!'

9. No-one tells you you're driving too fast.

10. You don't have to be nice to her stuck-up, snotty friends.

For her

1. You don't have to answer to *anyone*.

2. You can walk in the door after a *horrible* day's work, throw your clothes in a pile, flop down in front of the telly in a disgusting, food-splattered dressing gown, and eat rubbish while watching rubbish – without anyone surfing the channels just when it's at the good bit. ➤

3. Fat days seem less important. So long as your stomach's flat by Friday night, who cares if you're bloated on Tuesday?

4. You can talk on the phone all night about absolutely nothing and lie outrageously about how wonderful Susan looked in her new outfit without someone saying afterward, 'But you told me she looked like mutton dressed up as lamb.'

5. You can change your mind every five minutes, just for the hell of it.

6. You can masturbate to fantasies of the gorgeous workman you passed on the way to the office, without feeling guilty.

7. Everything smells clean and fresh. There are no lingering boy smells (the obvious mixed with cheesy socks, all vainly disguised with bad aftershave).

8. You can make your own smells – without feeling 'unladylike'. ➢

9. You don't have to explain why it's essential to own 25 pairs of black shoes.
10. You can get drunk and sob over your hated-when-sober ex – without feeling totally silly the next day.

THE MEET MARKET: WHERE TO FIND MR OR MS PERFECT-FOR-YOU

You see them. You want them. You get them. It's a simple equation that somehow doesn't always add up in the real world. For a start, most of us tend to get stuck on the first bit – actually meeting someone we'd like to go out with.

Someone once said to me, 'If you're not meeting the right person, you're mixing in the wrong social scene.' There's probably a grain of truth in that. After all, if you're looking for a conservative academic with family values you probably won't find them snorting coke down the back of a seedy nightclub. But you might well bump into them outside because, truly, you can meet someone anywhere at any time. Not just on the nights when you 'go out'.

'Where are all the single men?' women wail.

'Where are all the single women?' men moan.

Now, unless all singles are agoraphobics and refuse to budge from their own living rooms, it's obvious you're crossing paths at least some of the time. Nightclubs and bars aren't the only places singles hang out. Why not try . . .

> 'Once you've had your heart broken a few times, you're much more careful. I tend to break up with men pretty early unless I can see a lifelong future together. I don't want all that pain again.'
>
> Nikki, 22, sales rep

Parties

When you're feeling fab and looking terrific meeting people at parties is a cinch. Not so when you're frumpy, frazzled or the competition is hot. But it's worth making an effort because parties force people to spend at least a few hours in one place out of sheer politeness. So you've got time to sit back and study your target, watch who they're talking to and for how long.

They're being chatted up by a girl with legs as long as a giraffe or a guy who's so bloody good-looking he must be gay? They could be brain-dead boring for all you know. (You, on the other hand, have personality and lashings of style.) So find whoever organized the party and do some sleuthing. Single or attached? Nice person or steer-clear material? Find something you both have in common, then get them to introduce you.

'X, you must meet Sarah/Simon. They're as addicted to the movies as you are.'

The host/ess is snogging someone they've just met in the corner? Find an excuse to do something near your target – change the CD, grab some nibbles or enlist a friend's help and just go and stand over there. Next, simply catch their eye and smile a few times. If they seem friendly, close the gap and introduce yourself. Once there, flirt like mad, completely monopolize them and don't even think about going to the bathroom if the competition is hovering like vultures. (If you must, offer to get them a drink so you can come back to claim them.)

Top tactics

- Smile. Happy people attract people to them.
- Start a conversation. How do they know the host or hostess? What do they do for a living?
- Give them a compliment. Your friends have just voted them best-looking guy/girl at the party.
- Drop lots of clues on how to find you again in case you get separated. Where you work,

the suburb you live in, the fact that you know so-and-so.

No-nos

- Don't give up if you smile and they don't smile back. They might not have seen you (were too vain to wear their glasses) or simply drifted off in la-la land.
- Don't get drunk before meeting them.
- Don't muscle in when they're obviously already chatting up someone else or attached.

Nightclubs

In all the years I've been single, I estimate I've been to at least 50 different nightclubs around ten times each. Out of those 520 attendances, I've spoken to and flirted with hundreds of men. But you know what? I've only ever had a relationship with one that lasted past two dates.

'You're kidding!' said my girlfriends, when I

revealed this astonishing fact. *Silence.* 'But dead right – I've never ended up having a relationship with someone I've met in a club either.'

The stats back me up on this one: less than four per cent of people who meet in a nightclub, on holiday, or through the personals end up marrying. Subtract the other two and it evens out to one out of one hundred.

But there are nightclubs and nightclubs. I'm talking the dimly lit, music blaring, dance floor, can't-talk-unless-you-shout type. Clubs with cosy little bars off to one side and fabulous fresh-air outdoor drinking areas are a little different. For a start, you can actually see each other – and you can talk without all the veins in your neck popping out (most unattractive). So unless it's casual sex you're after, avoid the dark spots. Like your mother said, stick to the well-lit areas if you want to play it safe.

Top tactics
The dark bit: Anyone you meet after 12 drinks will seem wonderful. Don't give your home phone number to anyone you meet after three stiff spirits, work number only after you've downed up to five. (Get theirs if you're still able to talk after this and be sure to write a description to jog your memory the next day: 'girll who waz druk with fizzy hare' or 'blok wat tried to kizz me'). Whoever you meet, assume they're half as attractive as they appear under dim light. Don't expect anyone to call when they say they will and it'll seem a nice surprise if they do.

The lit bit: Be 50 per cent more suspicious than you would normally (the vibes from the dark bit leak out under doors). Use the flirting techniques described later in this chapter, especially the ones that make you stand out from the crowd. Don't wear black. Nightclub gear is more uniform than McDonald's.

Pubs and bars (minus the dance floor)

Now we're talking – especially if it's a pub. The combination of a packed crowd, plenty of chance to take the long way round and accidentally rub your way through the best-looking group in the place, a few ales to take the edge off, not too noisy so you can talk but noisy enough where silences don't seem uncomfortable . . . The only thing that could possibly make it better is a pool table. Personally, I would rather eat 12 hot chillies than pick up a pool cue, but I have to admire people who work the table: the old 'lean forward to show off the cleavage' if you're a girl; the 'push the cue really hard with your shirt sleeves pushed up so your biceps flex' if you're a bloke. We know what you're playing at guys (and it isn't pool) but the floor show works anyway!

Top tactics

Use the same formula as you do for parties. Move closer to whoever you've got your eye on. Smile a lot, make eye contact, make sure you're standing at the bar when they are. 'A bit crowded, isn't it!' or, 'Phew! Hot in here!' is all you need to get the conversation rolling.

No-nos

It's very easy to get carried away when you're drinking in 'shouts'. If you find you're singing 'Can't Get No Satisfaction' at the top of your lungs, you've had too many (and need to update your CD collection). Tip for male pool players: a bulging erection pushed into our back as you're 'helping' us is taking things too far, too soon. Doing that aggressive macho sulk thing when you lose isn't attractive either.

The friend-of-a-friend

This is how most people meet the love of their life – they're introduced through a third party (most often your family or a friend). A cinch when it's someone you know well – not so easy when you've seen them over at your neighbour's or at a distance at a sort-of-friend's party but never got to meet. You're too shy to ask them to set you up but if you don't act soon, you fear they'll be snapped up by someone else. Take a deep breath! There's nothing desperate about calling your friend or neighbour and saying, 'X looked cute. Are they single? What are they like?' A gracious friend will immediately offer to set you up (assuming they're worth being set up with!). If they don't suggest it, you do – and remind them often until they're so sick of you hassling them, they finally do arrange that drinks party.

Don't play it coy once you finally do meet

face to face. Sure, they might have figured out it isn't a chance meeting, but so what? If they're not flattered, they're not interested. Talk to them, pay them lots of attention and make it blatantly obvious you're interested, but leave the ball in their court to arrange another meeting. You've done the hard work – if they don't pick it up from there, the attraction's one-way (yours).

Top tactics

- Flirt but don't be *so* easy-to-get you remove all challenge. Once you're convinced they've got the green light to ask you out, cool it a little. You're inter-ested – but not desperate.
- Make sure the person who organized the meeting has your phone number (better still, give it to the person you really want to have it at the end with a simple, 'Call me if you'd like to').

- Call to thank the person who set up the meeting, but go easy on the 'What did you think X thought of me?' questions. You'll put them in an awkward position if the answer's, 'Not much.'

No-nos
- Friendly doesn't mean frothing at the mouth. Resist giving thumbs-up signs to involved parties when they're not looking (they'll catch you for sure). Pretend you're talking to your best friend and keep it light.
- Don't ignore everyone else in the room. You don't need to superglue yourself to their side.
- Don't hassle the person who got you together if they don't call you afterward. And don't run them down them either. It's not their fault they didn't fancy you.

A class

Someone once told me to sign up for a course that usually only attracts men. Brilliant idea, I thought, and trotted along in heels and a LBD (little black dress) to 'Basic Mechanical Skills Part I' at the local college. There, sitting around in their woollies and (where did they find them?) polyester slacks with permanent creases down the front, were all the nerds that lived in my area. Because let's face it: any *real* man who doesn't know how to check the oil and water isn't going to completely humiliate himself by admitting it in front of a bunch of strangers.

I was unlucky but that doesn't mean you will be. Night courses, especially, are a great idea. Two friends have 100 per cent success ratings: one did a Thai cooking course, licking more than the spoon after school. Another signed up for an 'Internet for People Who Still Use Pencils' course and landed herself a cuddly, bald but totally adorable uni lecturer.

Top tactics

Everything from 'I didn't quite hear that last point, what did they say?' to 'Can you come over to help me with my homework?'

No-nos

Loudly chatting someone up so the rest of the class can't hear the lecturer. Some people actually enrol to learn.

The office

Not surprisingly, around two-thirds of people meet their partners through work, because this is the one situation you know exactly what you're letting yourself in for. Not only do you spend most of your time at work, you get to check out how people perform under pressure (that is, you see the *real* them rather than a dressed-up, well-behaved version). Plus, there's a million opportunities to chat them up.

Top tactics

How to find out if they're single? Meet them first. It's easy. Just say, 'Hi, I'm Jo/John and I work in ——.' After a few smiles exchanged down the corridor ('How's your day going?' etc.) it's time to move in for the kill. Corner them in the lift or the coffee room or whatever, sigh, and say, 'What a week! I'm really looking forward to the weekend. How's your week been?' They'll answer, then you can drop in the all-revealing question: 'What have you got planned for the weekend?' If their answer starts with 'we', forget them immediately. 'We' never means their mother, dog or best friend, it means a lover/partner/spouse. Even if they don't drop the royal 'we', you'll get a big clue from what they do have planned. A few parties or clubs? They're probably single or not dating seriously. Renovating the house? Almost certainly attached.

Got the green light? It's easy to follow it up

with something like, 'I'm going to check out X (a bar or restaurant). Have you been there? Why don't you come along if you're not doing anything?'

If you don't want to be that forward and they work in your area of the office, ask them if they want coffee while you're passing their desk. Do they want to take ten minutes out to go *out* for a coffee? If they seem snowed under, offer to pick them up a sandwich while you're out. Next time, ask them if they want to have lunch at that great new lunch place.

No-nos
- Anyone who's married or in a serious relationship or your boss.
- Following them around, sending lovey-dovey e-mails, staring at them like a love-sick puppy dog.
- Flirting heavily (that is, snogging beside

the photocopier). Save it for outside work hours.
- Discussing the ins and outs (particularly the ins and outs) of your relationship with colleagues.

Your flat

You just can't believe it. For six months, you've shared the dishes, toothpaste and coffee. People keep assuming you're a couple because you do the shopping together, but it's a strictly flat-mate/friend thing – at least it was until now. Now you can't imagine why you didn't realize how stunning they were. Now you lie in your bed wishing you were in theirs across the hall. A gift from heaven – or the beginning of a nightmare?

Personally, I'd think twice before sharing a bed with a flatmate. For a start, you become instant de factos – the relationship's serious before it's even started. If you split up, one usually ends up moving out (leaving one of you with the problem of finding a replacement); if they don't move out, bringing home a new partner is never going to feel comfortable again. Having said all that, more than one married couple met when one answered a 'room for let' ad.

Top tactics

Don't act on impulse. Wait until you're absolutely certain you want to take the relationship further, then sit down and talk about it. Say how you feel and ask if they feel the same. If they don't, drop it (if you can't, move out). If you do decide to start dating, create your own 'space' for each other. Don't automatically sleep together every night. Keep going out separately with friends, in fact, go out *more*. In other words, don't live in each other's pockets even though you actually are.

No-nos

- Don't do it because you've just had an awful night where no-one chatted you up and you want reassurance that you're attractive.
- Don't do it because you're both drunk, you've just been dumped or your vibrator just died.

Introduction agencies

Oh no, has it really come to this? Hold on one second. You might be surprised who's using introduction agencies these days. Busy people. Career people. *Intelligent* people who realize they're unlikely to meet someone at a bar or a nightclub or don't have the time or energy. Isn't it logical to have a computer (because that's how it's done) match you up with someone with similar interests and aspirations? Sure, they can't predict chemistry but you never know your luck in a big introduction agency. Your 'how we met' story possibly won't thrill the grandkids but, truly, is it more dignified to say you met in a bar? Introduction agencies do the legwork so they're especially useful for people who are in their late thirties or forties when your options or avenues may have decreased. They can't promise miracles but a good, professional dating agency is well worth a try.

Top tactics

- Talk on the phone for at least an hour or so to make sure you're compatible. Don't be afraid to ask lots of questions: you both know you're after a long-term relationship so there's no

> 'This is the first time I've been single for any period of time. At first, it took a bit of getting used to and I was desperate to meet someone but I'm just starting to enjoy it. I met a really nice guy the other night and it was like, "Oh no! I hope I don't like you because I don't want to give up all this freedom just yet."'
>
> Lynda, 34, journalist

need to pretend you aren't.

- Arrange to meet for coffee rather than lunch or dinner so you don't waste time if it doesn't work. Be polite always but don't lead people on. If you don't like them, say, 'You're a great person, X, but unfortunately, not quite what I was looking for.'

No-nos

- Don't invite strangers to your home and don't go to theirs until you know them very well.
- If it's just sex you're after, spell it out. If you think that's all they're after, ask them.
- Trust your gut instinct and listen carefully to their relationship history. Are they using the service for the right reasons or because they really are such a no-hoper this is a last resort?

Dinner for Six

Dinner for Six and other 'meet new people' organizations like it deserve special mention. They don't bill themselves as introduction agencies but provide a way of 'supplementing people's social lives', in other words, a way to meet new people. They work because it's a big enough group not to feel obliged to be nice to one person in particular and small

'When you're single, you drive yourself more. You force yourself to go out when you'd really rather chill in front of the television. There's always this fear that if you don't make the effort, you'll have missed the one opportunity you had of meeting Mr Wonderful.'

Charlotte, 25, student

enough to get to know everyone reasonably well. A friend of mine went to a couple, and while he didn't meet the woman of his dreams, he made some great friends (who, I might add, were responsible for introducing him to his current two-year love). The more single people you meet, the more you up your chances of finding someone who's available that suits you.

Top tactics

By all means shine but don't dominate the conversation. If you see the person you're keen on being chatted up by someone else, don't panic, just move to sit next to them at the first available opportunity. It's totally acceptable in this situation to give your (work) phone number to more than one person in the group, even if they have obviously hooked up with someone else. You're there to make friends as well as possibly meet someone. In other words, even if you are hoping like mad they'll take it as a come-on, it's still considered polite.

No-nos

- Leaving after the entree because there's no-one there you fancy or particularly want to be friends with. Unless it's truly ghastly, it's polite to hang around until after the main course. Amuse yourself: try out a few funny dinner party stories to see if they get a laugh.
- Being openly critical: of the food, venue or the people. Just because you're not having a fab time, doesn't mean others aren't.

The personals

They used to be for men who couldn't go near a girl without tripping over their shoelaces and girls called Beryl and Marge who wore twinsets before they became fashionable again. Now people use them because there's no need for corny chat-up lines, nasty rebuttals and red, bleary eyes from smoke-filled bars. You can spell out exactly what you want from a partner, screen them over the phone and get to know them via the earpiece without ever having to press flesh.

But there are drawbacks. Be careful what you write in your ad and learn how to interpret other people's. It may come as a shocking surprise but not everyone uses the personals to meet lifelong partners: about 70 per cent are after sex. So keep it simple and steer clear of adjectives that could be misinterpreted (like 'fun-loving' – keen for casual sex). Give the basics of your appearance (tall, slim or short and petite) and that's it. Don't say 'lonely' or 'open minded'. 'Sexy' will only attract sleazes. If you're a professional person, say so, but don't advertise your income unless you want someone who wants a free ride.

Top tactics
As per introduction agencies, spend as long on the phone as possible.

No-nos

- If you decide to meet them, meet in a public place where you're known so that the person you're with can be identified.
- Take a friend with you first time around. Ask for identification.
- Stick to an area that's well lit with lots of people around.
- Give the details to several friends – where you'll be, the time you'll meet, the person's name, phone number and address.
- Never invite them to your home or go to theirs.

The Internet

There's got to be something in it or else the entire world would not be engaging in cybersex every minute of every day. This is when you go into a private 'chat room' and

> 'I live in the country and have a child so I find it difficult to meet people. One day, I was flicking through the paper and stopped at the personals. I thought, *Why not?*, then a little voice said, *Jesus! I must be a bit of a loser if I'm stooping to this.* But I gave it a go and I ended up meeting a really nice guy who I went out with for eight months. Another I went out with for two years. Pretty good innings really.'
>
> Judy, 35, single mum

type sentences like, 'Ummmm,' and, 'That feels great, baby,' very fast, using one hand. Not all Net nutters are after an intergalactic orgasm, however – plenty use their computer as a dating agency. All you do is call up a local dating site (or an overseas destination that appeals) and choose from the options available. There's everything from singles chat rooms to cybervow weddings on offer as well as an Internet version of the personals. Fill in a form on the computer, describe yourself, attach a picture if you like, then sit back and wait for the e-mails.

It's safe (no-one can track down where you live by your e-mail address) and, even I have to admit, bloody convenient. Once you've connected to someone you like, use the same rules that apply to personal ads and introduction agencies. In other words, chat on screen until you feel you've got a sense of the person. There are as many loonies (possibly more) on the Net as in your average nightclub so meet in a public place and tell people the details beforehand.

Top tactics

- Talk on the phone as well as through the computer. You can tell a lot about someone by their voice and phone manner.
- Buy a book about the Internet if you're a beginner. There are all sorts of strange codes you'll need to know: ☺ means

smile). If you want to come across as hip and happening in the chat rooms (and avoid saying yes to something you don't understand!), brush up on your Netiquette beforehand.

No-nos

- Don't lie about your appearance unless you never intend meeting in the flesh.
- Don't type in capital letters. Apparently, this is the equivalent of shouting. (I told you, this is weird stuff!)
- Also remember a lot of people use the Internet to shield shyness (the girl who's a scream on screen might get tongue-tied without her keyboard).

The chance meeting

They're in the queue at the deli, sitting alone in the next row at the movies, across the aisle on a plane, snivelling into a tissue at the doctor's surgery. It takes guts and confidence to front up to a complete stranger and the rejection factor is about 90 per cent (they're gay, married or just met the love of their life). But what have you got to lose? If they turn out to be the new lover of your best friend, get out of it by saying, 'I knew we'd end up friends!'

No time calls for drastic measures – especially if they're only going to be around for a few minutes. Swallow all pride (there's no way to get around this one without putting yourself on the line), walk up to them and say, 'Hi. I know this is ridiculous, but I've got the weirdest feeling we're meant to meet.' This will prompt either a warm, intrigued smile or a cold, 'Sod off, loony.' If it's a smile, follow it up with, 'Have you got time for a coffee or drink just so I can satisfy my curiosity?' Now, good looks and a tingly feeling in your tummy won't guarantee they'll turn out to be what you desperately want them to be, but at least you won't spend the next six weeks dreaming about a total stranger!

If they're trapped on a plane, train or bus, ask a question. Do they know which stop to get off at if you want to get to X? Where are the loos? Could you borrow their paper? While you're doing it, make it obvious you're looking for an excuse to talk to them. Smile every single time they look in your direction and look them straight in the eye. Bar writing 'Come and talk to me' in black felt pen across your forehead, give them a definite green light (and I wouldn't rule out the former if it's an emergency). You think they're interested but shy? Use the old 'haven't we met?' trick. 'Sorry I keep staring at you but you really remind me of my friend X, I don't suppose you're a relation?'

Places you just might get lucky include:

- **The supermarket**:
  Those new, wide aisles aren't for easy trolley access, they're for flirting in.

They're not talking about the food when they say, 'You can't get fresher than that' at Tesco's. Admittedly, you feel more confident date-hunting with a few stiff drinks under your belt than hovering around the Domestos in your tracksuit, but don't underestimate the supermarket as a potential hunting ground. Whether people add 'one blonde with big knockers' to their shopping lists is one thing but more than a few singles have connected while reaching for the same loo paper. Besides, you can tell a lot about someone by what's in their shopping trolley. Like, it's a pretty safe bet the man stocking up on nappies and tampons is married with child; the guy with chocolate biscuits and 25 frozen pizzas is most definitely single. Just one word of warning: couples frequently split up while shopping. Just as you're chatting nicely about Colgate versus Macleans, the other half comes thundering down the aisle clutching bread rolls.

- **The beach**: To be avoided at all cost unless you have a similar body type to Elle MacPherson or the new Levi's guy. On the other hand, if someone shows interest when you've got sand up your bottom, zinc cream up your nose and sweat dripping from every pore, they've got to be genuine. One word of warning though: never go underwater while on the pull. Stuff from your nose smeared across your face is not a good look.

- **The laundromat**: A terrific chance to check out their underwear without having to peel it off. Pick one which has a coffee shop just around the corner to satisfy both your caffeine cravings while your clothes are swishing around in the dryer.

Top tactics

- Don't be put off if they stare at you blankly when you deliver your come-on line. Simply repeat it. After all, their mind's not really in pick-up mode if they're in the deli tossing up between pastrami or the wafer thin turkey.
- Don't think too much. First, there's no time. Secondly, you'll never do it if you start worrying about making a fool of yourself.
- Can't think of one thing to say? Ask them *anything* to stall: the time, directions.

No-nos

- If they've got a wedding ring on, it's not on to approach them.
- Following them is also out – unless you intend catching up and saying something. They'll think they're either on *Candid*

Camera or see scenes from *Fatal Attraction* flashing before their eyes.

HOW TO FLIRT THEIR KNICKERS OFF (WELL, ALMOST)

It's a fact: confidence and a great sense of humour will score you more dates than good looks (though, I will admit, you're laughing if you've got all three). Chatting people up really is quite easy: all it takes is the right attitude and the willingness to take a few risks and make things happen.

Getting noticed

There are ways to stand out from the crowd *and* retain a sense of dignity. Attract his or her attention by using any (or all) of the following tricks.

Have a good time

Look around any crowded singles venue and you'll see groups of two (sorry girls, but it's usually us), their chairs facing outward, faces peering hopefully into the crowd, waiting for someone to come and talk to them. This sends two signals: 'I'm bored, come and entertain me' (hard work); or 'I'm desperate' (the supreme no-no). If you're smiling, laughing and thoroughly enjoying yourself, people notice. They think, 'I wish I could be with them. They're having fun.'

Attract attention

Pull out a Filofax or start writing intensely on the serviettes at a café and people have something to talk to you about. 'Is this going to be your first novel? What are you writing?'

Use the old 'look-then-look-away' trick

It's the best way to let someone know you fancy them without feeling like a twit if they don't fancy you. Look at them until they look back, then drop your eyes and smile to yourself. This says, 'I think you're cute but I'm too shy to come over.'

If you're with friends of the opposite sex, make it obvious you're not lovers

My brother and I were both single at around the same time and hung out together. Which was fabulous – but not so great when everyone assumed we were a couple. Bar wearing 'I'm her brother' and 'I'm his sister' badges (which we did consider), the only other thing that seemed to work was very definitely saying, 'This is my *brother*, Nigel,' whenever we were introduced to, or introduced, anyone.

Smile at them

If they pick up on it and smile back, great. If they look straight through you, move your glance ever-so-slightly over their shoulder and they'll think you were smiling at someone else. A smile can say, 'Come over and talk to me,' or simply, 'I like you and find you attractive.'

Make eye contact

Like the smile, this one's fairly foolproof and incredibly versatile. It doesn't matter where you are – in a café, on the beach (ditch the sunglasses) or buying sausages in the butcher's. All you do is catch their eye, hold it for a second longer than usual, then look away again. The more often you do it, the more likely they are to get the hint.

Don't worry too much about your opening line

People clam up when they see someone they fancy because they think the first thing out of their mouth has to be witty, charming or dead funny. It doesn't. A short 'Hot isn't it' or 'Great pub!' will do the job. Keep it simple and keep it logical. The best lines are often the obvious. 'Have you tried the chicken salad?' while you're standing in line at a sandwich shop. 'Do you know how to work this machine?' while you're at the gym.

Be impulsive and unpredictable

Most people aren't terribly creative so they're awfully impressed when they meet someone who is. It's not hard to be seen as unpredictable and wildly interesting. Thrusting a cold, frosty beer into an unsuspecting male hand while saying, 'Hi. My name's Lucy,' will be seen as highly impulsive and wonderfully eccentric. Telling a girl you love her earlobes will guarantee you a smile.

If you're not getting anywhere, take drastic measures

I'd fancied this guy for ages, but every time we met (he was a friend of a friend), he'd look straight through me. After trying every single ploy I could think of, I decided I didn't really care that he didn't fancy me, I just wanted to bloody well find out *why*. I plonked myself down beside him and said, 'So – why don't you fancy me? Are you gay, hate brunettes or just don't find me attractive?'

He burst out laughing and his flatmate piped up with, 'He *does* fancy you – he just didn't think you fancied him.'

We ended up going out for eight months. The point is, sometimes you really do have to take the bull by the horns.

If all else fails, blame it on a friend
'My friend and I have got a bet. She thinks you're a merchant banker, I think you're a writer.'

'My mate told me I wouldn't have the guts to come over and ask you if you've ever been on telly. Aren't you the girl in the toothpaste ad?' (Come on, we'd all love it!)

While you're watching them, they're watching you

The way you walk, what you're wearing, how you hold your drink (in all senses): make no mistake about it, you'll be judged instantly on all of them.

Make sure your clothes reflect the real you

A crotch skimming mini teamed with thigh-high boots will brand you a party girl (and that's putting it nicely) even if it is in fashion. A shirt undone to your waist, hairy chest and a gold medallion means womanizer (add crotch-hugging pants and women will start wearing garlic around their necks and making cross signs with their fingers when you approach them).

Not sure what to wear when you're out on the hunt? Two rules: wear something you feel comfortable in and make sure it suits the occasion. If in doubt, dress down rather than up. The girl who shows up at a barbecue, picking her way across the lawn in heels and stockings, instantly earns the label of 'pretentious snob'. A girl in jeans and a T-shirt is seen as carefree and down-to-earth when she's surrounded by standard black.

Feel desperate and you'll look it

Your biological clock is ticking like a bomb, you're dying to get over an ex, haven't had a date in ten years or simply having a fat day: those 'I'm desperate for attention' vibes send out waves that spread over a ten-kilometre radius. If you're walking out the front door praying to God this is the night, stay home. Murphy's Law guarantees not even the bar staff (and they're *paid* to be nice to you) will give you a smile when you most need one.

The better looking you are, the more work you have to do

This is what people automatically assume when they spot someone drop-dead divine. He thinks: *She'd never be interested in me/Bet her boyfriend's rich, powerful and built like a gorilla/What could I say that she hasn't heard a thousand times before?* She thinks: *Anyone that good-looking has to be vacant between the ears/Bet he's a bastard and really up himself/Bet he only dates models, he'd never go out with someone like me.*

The good-looking person is thinking: *Why doesn't anyone ever talk to me?/Why doesn't anyone ever ask me out?/What's wrong with me?* If you're above average in looks or have something particularly spectacular (a great set of knockers for instance), no-one will come near you unless you make it incredibly obvious you want them to.

If you're a confident female, some men will find you scarier than Godzilla

'Confident' in boy talk translates to any female who earns more than he does, has a more prestigious job, is more articulate, has a better sense of humour, is more attractive – and I'm really not kidding. A woman who knows what she wants and is confident of who she is, is as attractive as hell but requires a lot more courage to approach than your average girl (that is, six beers as opposed to two). If you're getting lots of looks but no action, this is probably what's happening. The solution? Smile a lot and look friendly. Or approach guys yourself.

Now you're talking . . .

OHMIGOD! They've taken the hint and on their way over. Relax, take a deep breath then:

Pretend you're talking to your best friend

Skip the small talk and clichéd 'do you come here often?' stuff and talk about what you normally would. Adopt a relaxed, friendly attitude even when you're screaming inside, 'God, they're *gorgeous*!' When you're both a bit more relaxed, then you can move into full-on flirting mode.

Don't leave your brain in the back seat of the cab

That LBD will be appreciated but you need more than a Wonderbra and great legs to keep someone's attention. Same for men. A jaw that looks like it's been carved with a chisel is what dragged us over but you need to open your mouth for us to hang around. A male friend of mine put it perfectly. Men are looking for a best friend with breasts. Someone they can share the good and bad times with – and bonk afterward. Women are also looking for a best friend with benefits.

Say their name three times in the first conversation

Repeating the name of someone you haven't met before not only shows you're interested, it makes them feel noticed and important. An added bonus: you'll actually remember it.

Give a compliment

But only if you mean it. Sincere flattery will get you everywhere. Insincere flattery sounds like a line (because it is).

Tease but not too much

Some people love a challenge and adore it when someone instantly takes up a contrary position to whatever it is they're talking about. If you're clever and articulate, go for it. Just make sure it doesn't turn into a slanging match where you're both trying to score points. Trading insults isn't sexy.

Make them laugh – but only if you've got a good sense of humour

Body language experts believe women should use more humour while flirting, men less. Why? Because men like to keep things on a more superficial level (and what better way than with a joke?), while women like deep conversations. Similarly, men laugh more among their own sex, women talk more and laugh less. It's something to think about, but if humour's not your strong point, don't push it. There's nothing worse than delivering the punchline and seeing a sea of expectant faces still waiting for it.

Be reasonably easy to please

The drink they bought hasn't got enough ice in it. It's too cold/too hot/too crowded/not crowded enough. Someone keeps bumping you. You can't hear them properly. Honestly, if it's that difficult, suggest going somewhere else.

Always leave when it's going well

Ahh, here she goes, sounding like those dreadful people who wrote *The Rules*. I don't mean to, but any performer will tell you you should always leave your audience wanting more. Flirting requires energy and 100 per cent undivided attention. Even the best flirt can only keep it up for a few hours – leave before you run out of steam.

FANCY A FLING?

Not all relationships last for ever – and neither should we want them to. A lusty three-week fling with a brain-dead but body-beautiful might be just what you need to get over that ex-obsession for good. The person who's cute and clever but about to be transferred to another city in three months? So what if the only aisle you'll walk down together is at the movies.

There are lots of different types of relationships and each has their own appeal. But you wouldn't know it. Most of us tend to divide relationships into two, mutually exclusive categories – serious (will end in marriage) or not serious (bonking and that's about all). There's also a perception that somehow you're 'wasting time' or 'being cruel' by dating someone when you know it's not going to be long term. Silly. Really silly. As long as you're honest (and not pretending to think white picket fences), there's absolutely no reason to refuse a date on Saturday night just because you know it won't last past a week. In fact, I thoroughly recommend it. Not just because first impressions are often wrong (and that one date can turn into a lifelong love) but because relationships are like everything else in life. Practice makes perfect.

The more people you go out with, the more you get to hone those relationship skills. The more diverse the people you date, the more likely you are to know exactly what type of personality suits you best. A just-for-the-hell-of-it fling is good for the heart, soul and spirit!

Date outside the square

I once went out with a man who was dead-set perfect 'marriage material'. Nick was tall, good-looking and earned enough money to single-handedly rescue all Ethiopian orphans. He was polite, stopped to pat dogs and children and wouldn't *dream* of parking in the disabled spot even if he was ('There's always someone worse off than you'). I dutifully ditched my slit-to-the-thigh numbers for the sort of clothes Nick preferred (conservative co-ordinates), spent my money on facials and manicures instead of wine and ciggies and hosted terribly proper dinner parties without ever forgetting to scoop my soup from the opposite side of the bowl. A few months later, as I reluctantly pulled on yet another blah beige ensemble, I suddenly thought, *What the hell am I doing here?* I was going out with a guy who did zilch for me, pretending to be someone I wasn't, simply because he was Good Marriage Material. And guess what? I didn't even want to get married! I dumped him quick smart and ended up going out with a totally unmarriageable (and rather nutty) psychology student. He made me laugh more in one week than Nick had in three months.

Like every other female I knew then, I'd fallen prey to the only-date-men-who-could-be-prospective-husbands trap. I wised up quickly after that. Long-term relationships and marriage aren't just about salaries and stability; they're about liking someone, chemistry and 'clicking'. What's right is what feels right for you *right now*.

I'm not suggesting we date everyone who asks us, but I am suggesting you open your mind and your Filofax to someone you probably don't want to share your room with at the old people's home. Date outside the square. Don't stick to the same type over and over. They seem a little out there? Give them a chance – you're going for a drink, not about to bear their children. The more motley your collection of exes the better – it shows you're adventurous and open enough to step outside your personal square.

Great reasons to play the field

- **You build a rather useful network.** Need your car fixed? Call the mechanic you once dated. Your computer's playing up again? That nerdy tech-head comes in very handy.

- **You can't have a serious relationship right now.** You're not ready for (or don't want) one but you do want someone to have fun (and sex) with? So long as you make this perfectly clear to your partner, there's no need to feel guilty.

- **You've just recovered from a long-term split-up and are easing back into dating again.** Resisting the urge to replace one long-term partner with another immediately means you'll give yourself time to work through the fall-out properly.

- **You aren't sure what sort of person would suit you long term so you're dating as many different types as**

possible. Bravo! The best reason of all!

- **You haven't kissed (let alone had sex) for six months**. Assuming you're not grieving for a past relationship or person, haven't been in intensive therapy or intensive care or haven't just been made managing director of your company, that's way too long without erotic contact. It's fling time – get out there!

Good reasons not to even consider it

- **To boost your self-esteem.** Even the word 'fling' sounds jaunty – and it's meant to be. You're there for fun and games, not deep psychological stroking.
- **To get back at someone.** Sleeping with your ex's friends won't show the arrogant so-and-so a thing or two – it'll just convince them you're still heartbroken.
- **Because you feel pressured into it.** Don't listen to your friends, your family (or me

for that matter): if you're not ready or don't want to date someone, don't do it.

- **To ease the pain of loneliness.** A stranger in your bed, who doesn't really care about you and you'll never see again, isn't the person to pour out your troubles to.
- **You don't honestly agree with no-strings sex.** If your morals or religion mean you'll wake up feeling 'dirty' and 'used' after sex that doesn't have a could-develop-into-something tag on it, stick to sex within serious relationships.

LOVE BITES . . .

Ever noticed how the talent looks better at closing time? It's not just the alcohol, say psychologists. We unconsciously inflate our opinions of others late at night to make ourselves feel better about the dwindling options. At 10 pm, singles judged the average attractiveness of opposite-sex club patrons as 2.3 on a scale of 1–5. Ratings soared to 3.8 an hour before the club shut. Unfortunately, the effect evaporates in the harsh light of the morning after.

Is stress stopping you from falling in love? Don't laugh – it could be. US researchers found relaxed female prairie mice were ready to commit for life within six hours of being 'introduced' to a new partner. Relaxed male mice spent a whole day deciding whether or not to stay. Subject the mice to stress and the scenario reverses: the male mice latched on fast and held on tight, the females dithered and took their time. Just how the researchers measured commitment in mice is rather intriguing, but since they've always mirrored human behaviour, it's another reason to stop either of you being workaholics!

Mr Right is No 13 – or so say researchers. They claim once you've experienced 12 relationships, you'll know what you want and who's best suited to give it to you. With No 13, you'll finally get it right!

Sick of trying to find your perfect match? In the year 2005, technology may do it for you. Hot Badges, tiny electronic devices that store and transmit info about your likes and dislikes, are set to become as popular as mobile phones. When you meet someone with a badge storing similar information, they both glow. The ultimate ice breaker!

Think twice before hitting the clubs in that mini and plunge top: it's nature's way of trying to get you pregnant. One bar and club survey showed single women's hemlines got shorter and necklines dropped during

*ovulation, your most fertile time of the
month.*

*Q: Why don't I ever get chatted up after a
break-up? Is it because I'm feeling
vulnerable and unconfident?*
*A: Yup. It's all to do with pheromones and
body language. When you're feeling up and
attractive (and especially if you're in the mood
for sex), your body lets off a musky scent that
others respond to. Your eyes sparkle, you smile
more, stand taller and project an air of
confidence. Yet another reason to curl up with
a video until you're over it.*

2

OK, I Think I've Found Them

•••

Y ou're intoxicated. You can't stop thinking about them. Images of them smiling/laughing/sleeping, flash up out of nowhere to dance in front of your eyes. A Mariah Carey song comes on the radio and *you don't switch it off*! Either you're 'in love' or you're experimenting heavily with party drugs.

Assuming it's the former, good for you! If you think you've found someone worth hanging on to, hold on hard. But there's something else you should also hold on to:

objectivity. Sorry to squash that soaring-above-the-clouds feeling but there's a long way to go before you're shopping for queen-size sheets and his 'n' her bathrobes.

This chapter shows you how to make it last when you've hooked up with the *right* person – and I know you don't want to even *think* about the alternative right now because it's like all your Christmases have come at once (or, more accurately, you've come so often it feels like Christmas). But it's not a *real* relationship yet. You're still in that goofy, 'You like me? Aww shucks!' first stage, and there are plenty of obstacles to dodge, jump or squeeze through before you're officially a couple.

Give yourself a head start by taking a look at how a typical relationship usually runs, so you can see where (hopefully) you're going, and what you'll need to do to get there.

THE SIX STAGES OF A RELATIONSHIP

While each and every relationship is unique, most move through the same love stages. If you're a typical couple, you'll probably experience them in the order I've listed; other couples may skip a stage and go straight onto the next. Or the opposite. If you've just found out your partner's cheated or work pressures keep you apart more than usual, you might slip *back* one or two stages before moving forward again. Whoever said the path to true love is never smooth was spot on!

Right now, you're in stage one: the gooey part. Arguably the best bit of all because you're both so idealistically optimistic, anything seems possible. Unfortunately, it's virtually impossible to stay in stage one for ever. Real life has an annoying habit of tapping you on the shoulder and saying, 'Excuse me, but don't you have friends, family and a job as well as a lover? How about some attention.' So you

67

both emerge, blinking in the sunlight (having spent the last few weeks in the bedroom with the blinds down), and the *real* relationship begins.

As with anything, knowledge is power. The idea of this section is for you to see how the average relationship progresses so you can get an idea of potential trouble spots you may be headed for, what's normal, what's not. But before you dive in, eager to see what's awaiting you, a word on the time frames I've used. They're estimates, that's all. We're all individuals and I'm generalizing horribly simply to give you a broad idea.

Stage 1: *yahoo!*
Timing: anywhere from date one up to three months

They're available and interested, so are you. There's chemistry both above and below the waist. You go out, you like each other.

Euphoria! Stage one is that lovey-dovey, soppy stage. You're reacting to primal instincts from your heart and your groin. You give each other those dopey grins. She spends a fortune on sexy new lingerie, he buys four new shirts. Where and how you met is a constant topic of conversation.

'I can't believe I didn't want to go to the dinner party,' he says. 'Imagine if I hadn't.'

'I nearly didn't go because my Mum was sick,' you say.

The thought of not having met fills you with dread. Life before them now seems dull and boring. The future is deliriously, ridiculously bright.

Sex

The only time you stop having it is when you lie back, snuggled in each other's arms, to talk about 'us'.

Keep it going

Treat them the way you'd like to be treated. Be yourself as much as possible. Don't push for intimacy too soon.

Check for

Chemistry: Does it *feel* right – do you fancy as well as like them?

Stage 2: fairytale fantasies
Timing: around two to six months into the relationship

In stage two, you still haven't found one thing wrong with each other; in fact, everything's just perfect. This is the heavy idealizing stage. You know enough about them to feel you know them well but you haven't been together long enough to see their faults, so there don't appear to be any. If a friend points out a glaring incompatibility (you're a brain surgeon, they're the cleaner; you want ten kids, they want none), you tell them, 'Have faith! True love conquers everything!' You lie to each other constantly. You force down hot curries because they love Indian; you sit through each other's favourite films and pretend you adore them. You hate spending even a night apart, and if you do, call each other three hundred times just to say, 'I miss you.'

Sex

It's still fun, fresh and exciting but a little less frenetic. Instead of having it twice a night, once is enough. Sometimes you even manage to eat first.

Keep it going

Let your heart rule your head but don't do anything rash (like get married or toss in your job to live in Saudi Arabia). Don't make long-term promises. It's okay to say, 'Wouldn't it be nice if this lasted for ever,' but not, 'Let's get married so it does last for ever.'

Check for
Compatibility: Do you share lots of similar interests, look at life the same way?

Stage 3: you officially emerge as 'a couple'
Timing: three to six months in
This is the bit where things start going wrong. The just-you-and-I-alone video nights are starting to wear thin – or your friends have threated to disown you if you don't come out with them – so you and your love venture out to be judged by others. You've met each other's friends before, but they now realize it's more than just a fling so look harder. And so do you. You start to see each other through other people's eyes. You watch your mum lift an eyebrow at his rattly old car and realize he earns

a quarter of what you do. Your best friend says, 'She's great – but I wouldn't have picked her as your type,' and you realize she's blonde and you only ever go out with brunettes. The lies start to be exposed: his childhood home's not quite the mansion he'd described, her ex couldn't possibly have been a model. You meet them at work and see a different side.

'A very old, very wise lady once said to me: you don't know if you love someone until you've seen through each season, twice over. This literally translates to two years but it also means going through the bad times as well as the good.'

Jeff, 26, chef

What's happening is this: you're both reconciling your glorified images of each other with a realistic idea of who you or they really are. Plenty of couples take the exit at this point when they realize the person isn't all they'd hoped for or find out they don't want the same things out of life. If you decide you do want to continue, you both drop the best behaviour act and feel safe enough to expose not-so-loveable sides, like a bad temper, insecurity, possessiveness and impatience. You start having a few arguments and question each other's judgement and opinions on things that really matter.

Sex
If you like the 'real them', sex shifts from the lusty, 'forget the bed, let's just do it right here' variety to a more loving, intensely romantic stage.

Keep it going
Don't panic when you discover your perfect lover's not so perfect after all. Give each other time to get used to the 'real' version, and you might just slide through. If it is obvious you've made a bad choice, however, now's the time to cool it. Split or agree to be friends.

Check for
Timing: Are you both ready for, and want, a long-term relationship? Because that's where it's heading.

Stage 4: why are you acting funny?
Timing: six to twelve months in

You're starting to think long term, so you start examining them with a microscope. In stages one and two you focus only on the good points; in stage four you focus only on the bad. 'You've changed,' you say accusingly. They haven't changed – you're just looking at them from a different perspective. Sometimes this is the end of what you thought was going to be 'the relationship': you can't move past the nit-picking or don't think it's worth it. Even committed couples feel a let-down. You're not as spontaneous. It's starting to feel familiar; maybe you're a little bored in their company sometimes. The arguments intensify as you both struggle for power and control. You drop almost all pretences: if you really are going to be together, there's no way you're eating sushi for the rest of your life. If you survive this stage, your faith in the relationship zooms higher. You know a major row doesn't mean you'll split up and you start to believe your partner actually loves *you*, warts and all.

Sex

You may be arguing more, which reduces the frequency, and differing libidos become apparent. It's around now you'll realize if one of you wants sex much more or less than the other.

Keep it going

Because you're arguing more frequently, planning a few good times is essential. Now's the time for a few relaxing, pampering weekends away from it all. Be honest with each other about what you're not happy with, but be tactful as well. Try to balance any criticisms with compliments.

Check for
Pace: Are you both 'fast' people and do things a million miles an hour or both stop-and-smell-the-roses people? The fights could be caused by mismatched energy and intensity levels.

Stage 5: the readjustment
Timing: around one to two years after you met
You both know exactly what you're letting yourself in for. You see each other as 'wholes' – good points and bad – and if the commitment's still there, start compromising on things you don't agree on. When people like me say you need to 'work on' your relationship, this is the stage at which you'll usually do it. Because

it seems likely you will stay together long term, you both take a careful look at the relationship to decide if it really is what you want for ever. You'll both need advanced communication skills to move further. You need to 'think for two', come up with win–win solutions to keep both of you happy, listen properly and be open about your needs.

Sex

You've established a pattern by now and settled into some sort of routine. If you've sensibly worked on your sex life as well as your relationship, you'll have reached some compromise on frequency and be able to let go of inhibitions without fear of being judged. If you haven't, sexual tension is starting to build. The low-libido person is feeling pressured; the high-libido person is frustrated.

Keep it going

You need to instigate *serious* discussion on what both of you want from life and relationships. Listen carefully and don't kid each other or yourselves. It's around now friends, family and perhaps your partner expect a deeper commitment like moving in or marriage. Make sure you're doing it for the right reasons, and not because it seems like 'the right thing to do'.

Check for

Common goals: Have you planned mutual goals for the future and are equally excited about reaching them together?

Stage 6: true commitment
Timing: three to five years from your first date

Whether you marry, move in or build a duplex, you make some sort of public statement that you intend staying together permanently. If it's a healthy match, you'll start to focus less on your relationship and more on your lives. You feel a deep, secure sense of satisfaction when you're with your partner but are equally as secure when flying solo. You hone your relationship skills to perfection. You can tell from across the room she's unhappy, simply by the way she's standing. She knows you're bored when you do that hand-through-the-hair thing. You feel comfortable sharing the most humiliating, embarrassing fears and don't criticize unless it's really important. You're kind to each other and there for each other. The bonds are strongest now: external events like the death of a parent, shattered career dreams, the realization that you won't ever earn a million/get your waist back may cause friction but it won't shake your faith in each other.

Each couple is unique in what true commitment and intimacy means to them. Some marry and never spend a night apart for the rest of their lives. Friends of mine say it's given them the freedom to separate for up to six months of the year, pursuing work projects on different sides of the world. Another very happy match have decided living together doesn't work. They rent apartments next to each other.

Sex

Your sex life reflects what else is happening in your life. If you have children, sex may be put on the backburner for a while (maybe even years). Ditto if something major happens – one of you gets a promotion or loses a job or a parent. Most couples drift in and out of great-sex and no-sex stages but if you've both given sex a high priority, especially since stage four, you're happy. You might occasionally yearn for new flesh but certainly aren't dissatisfied with what you're getting at home.

Keep it going

Love, respect and treat each other as the most important person in your life. Never take each other for granted. Remind each other constantly how lucky you feel spending your lives together.

Check for

You should be well and truly connected in all areas of life by this stage. All you need to do now is keep the communication lines open so you *stay* that way – for ever.

> ### LOVE IS A DRUG
>
> Why can't we stay in the really good 'in love' stage for ever? Some experts claim it's bio-logically impossible: our natural 'love chemicals' dry up after 18 months.
>
> When we're infatuated, our brain produces a range of intoxicating chemicals, ➤

says UK sexpert Sarah Litvinoff. Great sex (and lots of it) keeps the hormone surge fizzing. But in 18 months – around the time a Saturday night in's definitely lost appeal – the 'love buzz' chemicals run out and the 'in love' feeling disappears.

The most potent love chemical is phenylethylamine (PEA). There's also a snuggle-up chemical called oxytocin, which scientists believe is responsible for the urge to hug your partner so much at the start. As with any drug, the longer you have it, the more of it you need to get 'high' and the newer the love, the more chemicals produced. This could explain why love junkies swap partners: they're addicted to the chemical rush which is strongest at the start.

But if you do make it past 18 months, your body rewards you with another drug dose. This time it's endorphins: soothing substances that make us feel warm, content and peaceful. This is the stage when you can most trust your feelings, both biologically and ➤

psychologically (couples who get engaged around the two-year point have the best chance of avoiding divorce). In fact, the longer we stay with a partner and the happier we are, the more endorphins we release.

Help! My boyfriend's a perve!

There's the casual once-over and then there's the look that starts at the top and moves downward very slowly, very obviously undressing someone with your eyes. If your partner's checking out the talent using technique No 2, they're out of line.

It's a natural human reaction to look at really beautiful people, and admiring them doesn't mean you don't love your partner or are about to run off with them. But spending all night at a party chatting someone up and leaving with their phone number isn't okay. Even more exasperating is the guy who tries to justify outrageously flirtatious behaviour with the old 'but I was only being friendly and you're being insecure or jealous' comeback. It's like dog owners who say, 'He's just being friendly,' while Rover's madly humping your leg: it's bloody obvious Rover wants more than just walkies. If your lover's doing the human equivalent of humping but trying to make it seem like *you're* the one with the problem, he's being manipulative. Don't put up with it! Read the following to check you're not overreacting, then follow the fix-it plan underneath.

What's acceptable

- **Checking out other women when you're not around.** He knows a comment like, 'Look at the chest on that one,' is guaranteed to get him a slap on the back from the boys at the pub. It's pretty harmless if you're not with him.

- **Doing a double take when a girl walks in wearing a tiny skirt and so-small-it-could-**

be-a bikini top and has breasts the size of watermelons. You can't help but look at people like that. If some built-and-beautiful guy walked in with his shirt off you'd do the same.

- **Giving others compliments.** 'Sharon looks great tonight,' is fine. 'Sharon looks fantastic. It's a shame your legs aren't good enough to wear dresses like that,' isn't.

- **Lusting after celebrities.** Even if he dribbles while watching Cameron Diaz on video, it's not something you should feel threatened by. He's just expressing a healthy appreciation of the opposite sex. If he goes on and on about it, tell him it upsets you, and hopefully he'll just gaze adoringly at the screen rather than give a running commentary on how great she looks.

- **Catching your partner exchanging meaningful glances with a stranger across the room.** There's nothing essentially wrong with smiling at someone gorgeous as if to say, 'Yes, I find you attractive, too, but we're both with other people,' even if few of us enjoy seeing it. If it's not followed through by flirting, it's probably best ignored. After all, you probably do it too. It's an ego boost, a way of affirming to ourselves that we're still attractive and could pull a date if we weren't with our partner. If it seems like your partner's doing it deliberately, they might be trying to give you a good kick up the bum. It's the equivalent of saying, 'Hey! Don't take me for granted. I'm not cemented to your side, and other people find me attractive.'

What's not acceptable
- **Checking out other women in front of you.** If every female gets the once-over and he spends more time looking over your

shoulder than looking at you, take a trip to the ladies and don't bother coming back.

- **He's just started drooling over women when he didn't look twice before**. This is a danger sign. It can mean there are real problems in your relationship and he's subconsciously – or even consciously – thinking of leaving and moving into singles mode. Singles scan the room; happily attached people cast a lazy look around but it's not obvious. It could also mean your boyfriend's not getting enough sexually out of your relationship. If he's got a high sex drive and you don't, he might do a lot of mental lusting even though he wouldn't dream of acting on it. Therapists call this 'leaking': he's got sexual energy that's not being used up, it overflows and he starts fantasizing about other people. If you've been fighting a lot, also beware. When people are constantly criticized, they're very vulnerable to temptation. The message you're giving him is, 'You're not good enough.' He's looking around for someone who thinks he is.

How to fix it

- **Check with a trusted friend to make sure you're not being paranoid.** You can't expect someone to totally ignore all other members of the opposite sex, and if you put unrealistic restrictions on people, they will rebel. If you're unable to look at their behaviour objectively, ask a trusted friend and get their opinion. Are you overreacting or are they being an insensitive jerk?

- **If you're certain your partner's out of line, call them on it.** The standard answer is, 'You're jealous and overreacting.' Reply calmly. Say; 'No. I've thought about it and I'm not. I won't be treated this way. Look at other women when I'm not around if you have to, but don't do it in front of me. Serious flirting is out of bounds all of the time.' End of conversation.

- **Give him one more chance.** See if he's taken your feelings into account. If he hasn't and it happens again, repeat your speech and say you're giving him one more chance. Ask him, 'How would you feel if I'd been staring at that good-looking guy over there as long as you have the girl in the black?' It's underhand and stooping to his level but it will get his attention.

- **If he does it again, give an ultimatum.** This is one of few situations when an ultimatum is necessary – so give him one. Next time he does it, no matter where you are or who you're with, you'll walk out and the relationship will be over. Nothing he can say at that point will change your mind.

- **Follow through and leave if it continues.** He's had three chances to get his act together. If you've rationally and logically explained why you find it unacceptable and he chooses to continue, you're better off without the guy. Put up with him openly drooling over other people at the risk of losing respect for yourself.

Saying 'I love you'

They're the three most significant words in the English language. Deliver them at the right time to the right person and the first time they're said out loud calls for champagne. Blurt them out at the wrong time to the wrong person and you need a stiff drink for totally different reasons. It's the ultimate embarrassment.

Most of us have a justifiable phobia about being the first to say the 'L' word. Why? Because we don't know what the hell we'd do if our partner doesn't say it back. There is only one correct response to 'I love you' and that's 'I love you too.'

So, what if they say, 'That's nice. Anyway, as I was saying . . .'? Or look at you with pity and say, 'Sarah, you're awfully sweet but . . .'?

Timing is everything. Say 'I love you' too soon and you not only look desperate, you instantly lose power and dignity. Leave it too late and you risk missing that magic moment which could launch you both onto the next relationship stage. One couple I know have been in love for at least six months. I know it. They know it – but neither of them can get up the courage to say it to each other. They say things like, 'I really miss you. I really, really, *really* miss you,' and, 'God, I love being with you,' but you can see the frustration mounting. Sometimes, often, no other words but 'I love you' can express how you're feeling. (In fact, if they don't say it soon, I'll betray both their confidences and tell them what each other has said, in front of the other.)

So how do you judge when it's appropriate

to let the cat out of the bag? Only you can truly answer that one, but these are some things you might like to think about:

Make sure you both speak the same language

Your 'I love you,' might mean, 'I think this is special, let's give it a go.' His interpretation might be, 'When's the wedding?' If you think your partner will overreact, tack something on the end like, 'Don't panic – I'm not about to propose. I'm just telling you how I feel.'

Wait until you're absolutely bursting

Like, you'll explode if you don't say it right now. Wait until you're 150 per cent convinced you mean it. And no, you can't possibly mean it after three dates.

When I was 12, a kid at my school came up to me and delivered a message. 'See that guy over there?' he said, pointing to a kid from my

English class. 'Well, that's Brad and he sent me over here to tell you he loves you and wants to go steady.'

'Okay,' I said.

Brad and I went steady for a whole week. We didn't speak once though we did sit together outside E-block for a full five minutes and look at our feet. True love? You betcha! Telling someone you love them on the second date or second week is just as ridiculous. It's daft – and that's what they'll think you are if you do it.

The fact is, the first time anyone says, 'I love you,' they usually don't. Not really. True love takes years to develop and if you're lucky, it's always growing. You look back and think, *I really thought I loved them when I said it back then but it's nothing compared to how I feel now*. That's not to say you can't feel 'in love' after three months of heavy dating, and it probably is acceptable to trot it out then. For absolute maximum impact, I'd wait six. If someone says, 'I love you,' after you've dated for six months, they've thought long and hard about it. They truly do think there's long-term potential because it's often harder to say it later than it is earlier. Saying, 'I love you,' when you're in the infatuated part of the relationship is easy: you aren't aware of any faults. Saying it when you've got a pretty good idea of what you're letting yourself in for is far more of a compliment.

A much-loved ex of mine told me he loved me when I stumbled back to bed after throwing up for the sixtieth time that night because of food poisoning. Call me strange but I was far more complimented than if he'd said it across the candlelit dinner table earlier that evening, when both of us were tarted up and looking fabulous, totally unaware I was about to swallow a dodgy oyster.

If you're saying it first, sneak it into conversation

Who says it first? Whoever's bravest I guess. The coward's way out is to say, 'I *think* I'm falling in love with you.' If they look at you in horror, you can always say, 'Don't panic, I know it's just casual with us. I was only *kidding* . . .' or, 'That's why I've decided to break it off – you don't feel the same way.' Another less traumatic option is to pop it at the very, very end of a conversation when you can disappear immediately after saying it. Like just before you walk through the doors to catch a plane or at the end of a phone call. 'Love you,' then clunk. Dropping the 'I' off it also makes it less heavy. 'Love you' is what you say to your mum. Again, if they look uncomfortable, you can always add, 'As a friend, of course.'

If you're unsure of whether it's reciprocated, try putting something on the end of the sentence. 'I love it when you do that', 'I love it when we spend time together.' If they look wide-eyed and gaze at you hopefully, it's safe to say the big three words solo.

Don't ask them

Never ever follow up, 'I love you,' with, 'Do you love me?' If they do, they'll tell you immediately. If they don't, they're forced to say something like, 'Gee. Uhhh. I guess so.' Dignity demolished.

Don't do it with sex

Don't say it just before (especially before) or after sex – you won't be able to trust their reply. Some people will say anything to get laid, and if it's afterward, feel forced to say, 'I do too,' because they've just had sex with you, for God's sake. Few of us are courageous enough to ravage someone then say, 'Actually, it was just the sex I wanted.' Even if it was, they'll mumble something appropriate just to be polite.

LOVE BITES . . .

❗ *Drag this one out as a bit of trivia at your next dinner party. This is what palm readers* claim you can tell about your partner by looking at their hands.

- Will they be faithful? Check out the lines on the side of their hand, below their little finger. One deep groove signifies commitment; the more grooves the more easily tempted they are.
- Have they got a high or low libido? If their ring finger's longer than their index, they have a high sex drive.
- Are they a giver or a taker? If you can see light through the gaps at the bottom of their fingers when they're closed together, they're giving. If no light shines through, they're more selfish.
- Will they be fun in bed? If the tip of their

thumb tips back, they're impulsive and fun. If it's straight, so are they.

Dating couples want to be adored; married couples want to be understood. Why the shift? Being uncritically adored feels great at the start but it's far more flattering to be loved warts and all when someone knows you well. Married people feel most intimate when partners see them as they see themselves.

I just called to say –
- 'I love you': *70 per cent of lovers have rung simply to say those three words.*
- 'It's over': *12 per cent have taken the coward's way out and ended it with a phone call.*
- 'Marry me': *2 per cent have proposed, or been proposed to, over the phone.*

First impressions do count. Scientists claim it takes between 90 seconds and four minutes to decide if we fancy someone.

Can't decide if he's right for you or not? Trust your female intuition. Scientists now say women who rely on gut instinct make much better decisions than people who rely on rationality and cold facts.

3

Getting Serious
. . . .

It's not just your imagination: it *is* harder to find and keep a good long-term relationship than it was in our parents' day. The divorce rate is soaring, infidelity has reached an all-time high, single-parent families are commonplace and almost everyone over 30 has seen friends swap wedding vows for a divorce contract. Given such gloomy statistics, it's surprising we're still dating at all! But despite the break-ups, the friends with half a dinner service and one of two matching sofas, there *are* couples out there who give the rest of us hope.

I spoke to a selection of them – all long-term happy couples – to find out the secrets to their success. It came down to the following five points:

1. **Talking things through and being 'heard':** Talking openly and honestly with their partner, knowing they're interested and listening hard, was listed as of number one importance in every single case. Being able to reveal all, without fear of being judged, is, in a nutshell, the secret of long-lasting love. If you get that right, the rest is easy.

2. **Commitment and trust:** These were also up there, with commitment defined as 'I know he or she's in it for a long time, not just the good times' and trust defined more as 'he or she will do the right thing by me' rather than faithfulness.

3. **Freedom:** All couples gave each other space to see friends and pursue interests

separately, but also made an effort to do lots together. They made time for their relationship and consciously planned pleasurable 'dates', away from work and chores.

4. **Support and friendship:** When asked what they most liked about their relationship, almost all the couples listed support as one of their top three reasons. 'She helps me and I help her – we guide and advise each other on our careers and our problems,' was a typical answer. Most had 'got over' that initial in-love stage, and while they still loved each other, companionship and the joys of having a 'live-in best friend' were as important as sex.

> 'He's the person I turn to when I'm in strife. I can do anything when we're together because he gives me strength and total support.'
>
> Carla, 23, shop assistant

'Because I love her so much, I'd rate my sex life as ten out of ten – though I've probably had better sex in a technical or lusty sense with other people,' said one happily involved man.

5. **Working at it:** Not one of the couples expected their relationship to coast happily along – all were prepared to put the effort in to get through the rough patches.

GETTING HIM TO OPEN UP

Relationships expert Dr Maryon Tysoe says one of the strongest binding elements between two people is their ability to reveal intimate thoughts and feelings to each other. She cites one study which tried to predict which couples would stay together over a four-year period by just one factor: how much they shared their feelings. The results were as expected: the more the couples shared, the ➤

more likely they were to be together four years on. Another survey of 400 therapists showed the largest single reason they thought marriages failed was the husband's inability to communicate his feelings.

Unless your guy's spent the last five years locked away in a dark room playing computer games (come on, he must have come out sometimes), he's probably got the message that he should be opening up. Then why doesn't he? Because deep and meaningfuls may not be that easy for him. Most women consider a good, long, deep conversation one of life's pleasures. It's up there with walking into your favourite designer's with a spare £500 to blow. For some men, a deep conversation isn't enjoyable at all because it's hard work. Men are 'doers'. When he meets up with the boys, they don't sit around in coffee shops chatting. They play pool, go to the football, go for a jog or the pub. He's not that practised at talking intimately so it requires effort. And say he stuffs it up? 'I worry I'll give the wrong answer.' ➤

'It all comes out wrong and I upset her.' 'I don't know what she wants me to say.' They're the comments I got from from male friends who don't find it easy to talk to their partners. If talking doesn't come naturally to him, it's not surprising he's all for going to the movies rather than out to dinner (where you're bound to want a conversation).

My idea of a good time is a good chat. My ex's idea of a good time was playing tennis. Personally, I would rather clean all the public toilets at Wimbledon, than hit a ball around the court. Why? Because that doesn't come naturally to *me* – I'm embarrassingly pathetic at it. My boyfriend would say, 'I know – let's have a game of tennis!' expecting me to jump up with an enthusiastic 'Yes!', rush into the bedroom and pull on a short white skirt. Instead I'd do *anything* (even watch football on telly) to avoid it. The last time I was forced to play a game of social tennis I spent most of the day before sitting on the loo. If a 'deep' conversation for men is ➤

the equivalent to tennis for me, they have my sympathy.

Unfortunately, being able to have an intimate conversation is slightly more crucial to relationships than perfecting a backhand. Besides, once they do get the hang of it, most men admit having a good chat is an incredibly rewarding experience. Which is more than I can say for tennis.

How to help him open up? Encourage him by:

- **Letting him know talking is important to you.** Say, 'I know you don't feel comfortable talking about your feelings just yet, but it would mean a lot to me if you'd try.' Explain why. Get him to read this section of the chapter and other sections in the book which talk about communication issues.
- **Rewarding even the slightest hint of intimate talk.** If he usually says, 'My boss, Bob, is a bastard,' then one day comes ➤

out with, 'I don't know, Sally, sometimes I think Bob isn't happy with my performance,' let him know you're thrilled. I don't mean jump up, throw your arms around him and say, 'Honey! At last! You're talking to me' (he'll clam up for good). The trick is to acknowledge it but not make a big deal. Let him know a) you don't think 'less' of him for revealing a fear; b) it's normal; and c) it's great he let you in. Say something like, 'I think all of us worry about that sometimes – I sure as hell do. What makes you think that?' Let him tell you, then say at the finish, 'I'm glad you let me know. It's nice to know how you're feeling.'

- **The more open you are, the more open he'll be.** If you're comfortable with talking about 'embarrassing' things – topics which make you look a bit foolish – he'll take your example.
- **Ask him questions.** If you think he's worried about something, say, 'Are you ➢

worried about this? Tell me,' then truly listen to his reply. Guide him along by saying, 'What did you feel then? Angry? Confused? Frustrated?' Yes, you are putting words in his mouth, but you're also teaching him *how* to talk intimately.

- **Don't assume silence means disinterest.** This is the main difference between how men and women talk: women tend to think out loud, men tend to work things through in their heads. He might mention a problem he's got ('My boss is really getting up my nose'). The next time he mentions it, you'll probably hear the conclusion ('I've decided to apply for a job with another company'). The middle bit – weighing up the pros and cons – he does privately. That's why, when you ask his advice about something, he might say, 'Let me think about it.' He's not fobbing you off, that's just the way he handles problems. Women, on the other hand, verbalize thoughts. In fact, we're rather ➤

fond of expressing *every* thought that enters our head, not just important ones. So we might say, 'Okay, I've got to go to the bank, then the drycleaners. No, I'll go to the drycleaners first because it's on the way. Jesus! I nearly forgot! I have to drop in that presentation to a client, even though it is Saturday. Honestly, sometimes I feel all I do is work, work, work. Where *is* that bloody black jumper? Oh – here it is. Brilliant. Now, darling, what do you want me to pick up for dinner? Darling? Honestly, I might as well talk to myself!' (You are.) Here's what he'd say in the same circumstances: 'I'll be back in an hour.' When he thinks or says, 'I wish she'd get to the point,' this is what he's talking about.

FOUR RELATIONSHIP NO-NOS

1. **Reminiscing about an ex during your special moment.** You're lying in bed watching the raindrops trickle down the

window pane when he says, 'This reminds me of the time Mary and I were lying in bed in this great little hotel in Ireland.' They know you've been around the block – spare them the addresses.

2. **Betraying each other's secrets.** You introduce her to your work colleagues. She says, 'Trevor was right: you *do* look like the woman out of *Two Fat Ladies.*' Anything derogatory said about friends, pillow-talk, those intimate, highly embarrassing childhood confessions: none are to be repeated.

3. **Criticizing when they're doing their best.** It might not occur to you to marinate the steak in gin or wash the chicken with detergent but he's doing his best. Let your partner have their big moment.

4. **Constantly apologizing.** 'Sorry honey, I shouldn't have said that/done that/breathed so loud.' Women seem to have far too many

polite genes. He knocks a cup of coffee out of your hands and you're the one who apologizes. Like, sorry for existing.

'Let's live together'

You're sick of trying to find something, then realizing it's at *their* place. You're tired of carrying a change of underwear around in a plastic bag. Suddenly it seems like a complete waste of money to be paying two lots of rent when you're spending every night at each other's place anyway. You love each other, the idea forms and then it's said out loud: 'Perhaps,' one of you says tentatively, 'we should think about finding a place together.'

Break out the champagne – you've officially moved the relationship forward about six million paces. But don't be too hasty: there's much more to moving in than finding a place to move into. Like, are you really sure you're ready to give up the courting bit just yet? 'One minute, we were dating – I'd doll myself up, he'd arrive on the doorstep with flowers – the next, we were flopped on the couch eating takeaways with greasy hair,' says Anna. 'We fast-forwarded through those fizzy, sparky bits into domesticity. I felt ripped off. I know it would have happened eventually, but it happened too fast.'

He sees you plastered in night cream instead of make-up; you see him out of his suit and trimming his toenails. Hardly the stuff of lust but all part of being human beings who can't look or act perfect all of the time. (One word of warning: don't get *too* comfortable together. It's okay to pull on the tracksuit some of the time but break out the glad rags occasionally.)

Apart from noticing what slobs you both are, you'll also notice a loss of privacy. It's one thing going out and spending just about all your time at each other's place. It's quite another officially moving in. Before, if you felt irritable or tired and fancied a night by yourself, you simply stayed home. Give up your own place and there *is* no time out from the relationship.

The first week or two of living together is heaven. You throw a house-warming party, feel all grown up, cook lavish meals for each other, snuggle in at night. Then you move into the 'who left the cap off the toothpaste' period and it's *hell*. There's a massive adjustment period for both of you. You might think you're 'one' but in reality, you're two individuals with different ideas on how to run a house and your lives. You'll fight about the housework, sex, general cleanliness, moan about money and who takes the rubbish out. Each of you will be struggling for power, trying to be the one who's boss. Which is one reason why I wouldn't suggest either of you move into the other's house unless it's so wonderful you'd need your heads read to give it up. Finding a new place together, with both names on the lease, puts it on an even power keel. 'It seemed obvious to move in with Maryanne because her place was bigger,' says Matt, 24. 'But I never ever felt like it was my home because it had always been hers. I think she also found it difficult because she was so used to living in the flat alone.'

Prepare, also, for a change in your sex life as first-time flatmates. Your sex life could improve dramatically once you move in – or fall in a big heap! 'After years of sneaking around corners – hiding from his flatmate or my parents – to finally be able to have sex somewhere other than bed was a fantasy come true,' says Leonie. 'Our sex life definitely improved when we moved in simply because we were free to make love when and where we wanted to.' Others couples feel somewhat differently. 'Jess and I definitely had more sex before we moved in because we'd grab the chance whenever we could. Now we know we can have it every night – and that's some-times a huge turn-off,' says Jake.

Merging lives isn't easy. *Expect* to argue, *expect* to feel resentful, sulky and irritable for the first little while and you won't be disillusioned. Give it a good four months before throwing in the towel (in the laundry basket, please!): it really does take that long to settle in.

Here are some things you might like to think about *before* rushing straight to the real estate agent, pens poised to sign a shared lease. If you can't agree on issues like this before you move in, you haven't got a hope afterward.

- **Spell out very clearly what moving in means to each of you.** Is it for convenience and a temporary thing? Is it because you want to spend the rest of your lives together? Is it a trial run to marriage? If it is, how long do you want to live together before tying the knot? Personally, I wouldn't advise moving in with someone unless the intention is to move the relationship a stage further on. If it's money problems that are forcing you to move in, get a flatmate – that's what you're truly after. It takes great tolerance to live with someone else and cope with all their personal habits. It's difficult enough when you're madly in love, let alone when you barely even like each other.

What furniture do each of you have? Can you stand living with each other's stuff? If one person's got designer taste and the other mismatched hand-me-downs, will you feel resentful? If the bad-taste partner doesn't mind, whack the not-so-nice stuff in storage for a year or so (and good luck deciding which of you has the bad taste). Don't sell it until then: you never know, it may not work out and that bright purple coffee table might come in handy.

Decide on what you need to buy and who's going to foot the bill. It's romantic to go halves on things like fridges and sofas, but a complete pain to split it all up if it doesn't work out. Instead, write down the items you need to buy and split the list. You buy the fridge, he buys the telly. You buy the dinner service, he buys the saucepans. If it doesn't work out, you take whatever you bought and there's no messy arguments over who owns what. If you're really sensible, you'll make a list of all your possessions, including books and CDs, before you move in. It's easy to forget who originally owned what.

How will you split expenses? Differing money styles can cause a few arguments when you're just going out, but neither of you have the right to criticize. Once you've moved in or start buying shared possessions, however, who's stashing cash and who's blowing it is important.

- **Can you afford to live together?** Sit down together and talk about your existing financial commitments. Can you both *afford* to split expenses evenly? Work out a budget plan. It doesn't matter whether you plan to keep separate accounts or not – household and entertainment expenses still have to be shared. (On the subject of sharing, also have a chat about how you'll split the housework!)
- **How will you handle friends and visitors?** Are you the sort of person who craves time alone while they're the social type? Do you have friends who are prone to drop in for a coffee, stay for hours and maybe even crash the night? How does the other partner feel about it? Set some rules for friends and visitors and stick to them.

WILL THEY EVER ASK/ACCEPT?

Not so long ago, it was the woman who'd be gazing longingly in the jeweller's shop window while he studiously gazed at the sports watches, refusing to even glance at anything remotely round or glittery. These days, it's just as likely to be *him* trying to drag *her* up the aisle. But there's one other thing you need to get married: a proposal. These range from the partner on one knee, serenading violins and diamond ring popped in a glass of champagne variety to the '"I suppose we should get married," muttered while you're climbing into your jammies about to go to sleep' sort. If neither are happening to you and you'd like it to, how do you bring up the subject of marriage without feeling like a desperate twit? I'm going to address this section to women, since it's still usually men who do the asking-to-marry bit, despite so-called equality. But most of the advice is applicable ➤

to both of you and I want to make something clear first: there's a perception out there that women get more out of marriage than men do. I'd have to agree women probably get more excited about the wedding *day*, but once all the hoo-ha dies down, men actually get a lot more from marriage than women do. Most surveys show the two happiest groups of people are single women and married men. Men are also much more likely to want to stay married. In one survey, husbands and wives were asked if they'd marry each other again, knowing what they do now. Fifty-six per cent of women said yes, compared to 71 per cent of men. Married men drink less, take fewer risks and live longer than single men. Men take much longer to get over a divorce than women do. Ironic isn't it? Here you are reading this, hoping it'll result in him on bended knee, when he's the one who's most likely to benefit from it.

Anyway, here's my advice on working ➤

out where your partner's head is regarding marriage, without losing dignity.

·First, look at your own motives for the conversation. Are you bringing this up because you want some idea for the future or because you want a commitment NOW? If you'd simply like some feedback because you're curious and deciding whether to hang around long term, just say, 'I was reading a story/watching a TV show and it started me thinking about relationships. What do you think about marriage? Can you see yourself doing it someday?' Get some feedback, then switch topics ASAP. If you want to continue the discussion make it very clear you're talking about marriage in theory, not the two of you skipping off into the sunset.

You're hoping the discussion will end with a proposal? Check you're up for it before going any further. Are you really ready for this? Have you been together at least two years? Are you wanting it for the right reasons? Do you honestly think your life ➤

will be enriched 20 years on from now by being with this person? Do you honestly believe they feel the same way about you? Once you're satisfied *you're* sure, work out your own theories on why they haven't asked you already, before putting your partner on the spot. That way you're prepared and able to talk logically rather than emotionally about the issue. Be honest with yourself. Could it be they haven't asked you to marry them because they're not ready or not sure?

· **Introduce the topic.** Personally, I'd be up-front about this one. You're better off being honest than sending out subtle signals. For a start, most men don't pick up on subtleties, so looking at him wistfully during the gushy proposal bits in movies won't get you anywhere. If you know each other well and talk openly and honestly (and if you don't, you're not ready to make plans for next Christmas, let alone the rest of your life) wait until you're having a particularly good time together and introduce the topic generally. ➤

Start with the same point I mentioned previously – something like, 'I was reading a story/watching a TV show and it started me thinking about relationships. What do you think about marriage? Can you see yourself doing it someday?' But this time, follow it up with, 'Have you ever thought about *us* getting married?'

His response will be one of three. The first: absolute horror. If he shoots you a 'you've got to be kidding' look, forget it – and him if you want commitment. This guy's either deleted the 'm' word from his vocabulary or you're definitely not his idea of Ms Right. The second reaction is one of confusion. He hasn't really thought about it but that doesn't mean he won't in the future. All you need to say then is, 'I'd like you to think about it because I'd like to know where we're heading.' Unless you're planning on doing the proposing your-self, drop the subject right there. Let him think about it for a few months and see if he wants to take it further. ➤

If you've been together for ages, the third reaction is probably the one you'll get: he has considered it but he's not ready right now because of – whatever reason he has. Resist the urge to jump straight in with, 'Oh, for God's sake, that's ridiculous! I don't care if you haven't finished your law degree/built up a bank balance/still live with your mother. Let's do it anyway,' because it really doesn't matter how trivial *you* think the reason is, it's important to *him*. You'll get a lot further with, 'I understand where you're coming from but just for the record, it's not important to me.' If you're prepared to wait for whatever it is he's waiting for, again, stop it there. If you're not, you'll need to add another sentence onto the previous state-ment: 'And John, I'm really not happy to put our plans on hold for another five years, so could we talk about this further?' Have the discussion, then:

· **Ask for a time frame** of when he'll be ready to commit, then set your own – the maximum ➤

amount of time you'll wait for him. Tell your boyfriend you're giving him six months, a year, whatever, to make up his mind. Don't issue it as an ultimatum; simply say, 'John, we've been going out three years now and I'm asking you for a serious commitment. I love you but marriage is important to me. I'm prepared to wait another [whatever] but then I'd like an answer.' Drop the subject but stick to the deadline.

· **Mark the date in your diary** and let him know a week or two before D-day. If he comes up with a good reason not to commit then, you might want to reconsider. Then it's up to you to decide whether he's worth another wait or not. If you decide he is, mark another date in your diary and make it your personal deadline. Tell him. If he won't commit then and you still need that commitment, it's time to move on. You've given it your best shot but it just isn't going to happen. Hang around after that, and you could be waiting for ever.

LOVE BITES . . .

❗ *The term 'settle down and get married' is truer than you think.* Men's levels of testosterone (the hormone which contributes to aggressive, dominating behaviour) test high when they're single, drop when married and rise again on divorce. Other research shows alcohol and drug use decline in both sexes after marriage, probably because it encourages a sense of responsibility. Live-in lovers don't alter their lifestyle habits and neither marriage nor moving in stops smokers lighting up.

❗ *Thinking of getting married after years of living together?* If you're doing it because all your friends are, your friends and family want you to, you think it'll fix your relationship problems or simply because you want to have kids, you're on the way to *joining the 50 per cent of couples who split within five years once they become Mr and Mrs.*

Q: What's number one on most people's prospective partner list?
A: Being able to make each other laugh.

'Will it last?' is the most common question couples ask during premarital counselling – and just about all think love is the crucial ingredient. Wrong. Liking each other – sharing feelings, talking and feeling supported – is the most essential quality. Researchers rate passion as number two and being 'good friends', the third. Interestingly, passion decreases over time for women, but not for men.

What was that about gay relationships being short-lived? In Denmark, where it's been legal for same-sex couples to get hitched (and unhitched) since 1989, the divorce rate of Danish homosexuals is 17 per cent compared to 46 per cent for heterosexuals.

> **!** Sure, you spoil each other rotten on birthdays, but you'll last longer if you celebrate lots of milestones. Keep a record of significant dates and mark each as an anniversary. It keeps you focused on the positives.

4

Sex: The Glue Which Sticks You Together
••••••••••••••••••••••••••••••••••••

'To tell you the truth, Trace, I'd much prefer to read my book,' said my boyfriend of three years, lifting the duvet to peer down at me.

Call me sensitive, but when you've got your mouth wrapped around some guy's penis, it's rather insulting to be told to stop. It's sort of like a shivering street kid holding up the fur-lined leather jacket you're offering, when it's snowing and minus 30 degrees, and saying, 'What, *this*? I wouldn't be seen dead in it!' Mustering up all the dignity one can when

forced to emerge, *un*triumphant, from the
darkness, I tried desperately not to be offended
at being passed over for Jeffrey Archer. I failed.

'Sorry, honey, what was I thinking? I forgot
we'd had sex once this month already,' I
snapped.

'When are you going to grow up?' my lover
(actually, scratch that and make it 'roommate')
retorted, waving the hated book madly about.
'Honestly, we're not 17 any more, in case you
hadn't realized.'

No. Twenty-eight – practically in our graves.

'*No-one* has sex all the time when you've been
together as long as we have,' he said with that
superior 'I'm trying very hard to be patient'
look.

'John and Alice do,' I ventured.

'Phhhhtttt! You're holding *them* up as an
example!!!! The couple who *tongue*-kissed in
front of our guests at the last dinner party?
They're . . . well, they're . . . sex maniacs!'

I knew there was a reason why I liked them so much.

'Perhaps,' said the about-to-be-dumped-big-time boyfriend, 'you'd be happier living with *them*, if you think they're so great. You can all have a . . . a threesome or . . . something.'

Actually, that's not a bad idea, I went to bed thinking (the living with them bit, not the threesome). And I did shack up with John and Alice (though, I hasten to add again, not in the sense *he* meant) for a month until I found another flat. Solo this time. That way I could have sex as often as I wanted to, even if it was just with myself. Funnily enough, I'm still friends with John and Alice but appear to have lost contact with Mr Sex-is-for-Teenagers. After all, us sex maniacs have to stick together, and anyone who expects it more than once a month (I really wasn't joking), obviously qualifies as one. Not.

At this point you're (hopefully) having a bit

of a chuckle but maybe feeling a tad guilty as well. Like, you can sort of identify with the wanting-to-read-rather-than-bonk bit? Relax! It really is normal. *Everyone*, even that hussy who works in the off licence and licks her lips and thrusts her chest out at *anyone* in trousers, occasionally thinks, *If I have one more fag maybe he'll give up and start snoring.* She, like you, isn't always as eager when she's shagged out from carting around one-too-many cartons of beer.

But – and it's a BIG but – while it's okay to give an exaggerated yawn now and again when your partner turns to you with that un-mistakable twinkle in their eye, constantly and consistently saying no to sex is not a good idea. For you, them or the relationship.

Making love isn't a luxury, it's essential for your relationship to survive. According to research, we get about a quarter of our total enjoyment of a relationship from sex. That's if you're having *good*, regular sex and the rest of your relationship's in pretty good shape. If you're having bad sex, or none at all, the other three-quarters of the relationship that *was* good, gets cancelled out. Why? If your sex life is in drastic dire straits, it spills over into the rest of the relationship and ends up poisoning everything.

Stop having good sex and you stop feeling connected to your partner. If someone doesn't want to make love to you, you don't feel sexy or attractive. Your self-esteem plummets. Sexual frustration makes you irritable. Resentment means you start getting angry over things that previously didn't worry you. Without sex, intimacy disappears. Both of you feel increasingly isolated. You start fantasizing about other people. You may take it further and actually have an affair. Or you might just up and leave.

Bad sex really is bad news. Put the relationship first and sex last and you lose the most effective way of nourishing yourself and each other. Give it the same importance as the relationship itself and everything falls into place much more easily. I'm not saying you should expect great sex *all the time*. Sometimes career and children have to take priority, and all couples go through phases when sex isn't as good. Just don't ever give up on *trying* to make it as good as humanly possible.

Here are some hints, tips and tricks to inspire you along the way!

FIVE STEPS TO A GREAT SEX LIFE

Sex is a bit like typing. Anyone can sit down and bash something out using two fingers, but you'll never be as good as the person who uses ten and took the touch-typing course. This quick step-by-step guide is the equivalent of the touch-typing course (except a hell of a lot more fun). Once you're firmly established as a couple, it's a good idea to work through the following programme to set up a strong foundation for your sex life and open the lines of communication. You don't have to do this in order, just pick whichever suits the mood at the time.

1. Put it on paper

Each of you grab a notepad and pen and write down, being as specific as possible, what you do and don't like about your sex life. You can do this together or separately, but no talking as you're writing!

Divide the page into sections with different headings: 'What I need to get in the mood for sex'; 'What I'd like more or less of during fore-play/oral sex/intercourse/during orgasm/after sex'. At the bottom write general comments: are you happy with when, where and how often you have sex? Are there any new things you'd like to try (acting out fantasies, sex games like tying each other up or renting an erotic film)? Also include relationship issues: what you do and don't like about the relationship, areas you think need work. Be as honest as you can but be a little tactful. Try to think up as many positive things as criticisms, and word it carefully. 'I'd like more foreplay,' rather than, 'You don't give me enough foreplay.'

When you've finished, it's not a case of swapping lists and skimming to see how you rated as a lover. Instead, read them to each other, talking through each point as you go along. Obviously, the best time to do this is when you've got time to talk and both of you are in good moods. Attempting it after a weekend with your mother (lovingly nicknamed 'that old bitch' by your partner) is asking for trouble. You'll be crucified. So pick your time. One goes first, then swap. Try to be as clear and non-judgemental as possible when you're talking. Saying, 'I hate it when you're too rough,' is guaranteed to make your partner prickly. Saying, 'I like it when you're really gentle,' (even if they never are) is a nicer way to give them the hint.

When both of you are finished, each summarize what the other has said so there's no room for miscommunication. The more specific you are during the discussion, the more you'll get out of it. Saying, 'I'd like intercourse to last longer,' isn't enough information for him. You need to spell out exactly *how much* longer, or he'll still be thrusting away six years from now after buying a lifetime supply of Stay-Hard-Forever.

Give each other a few hours to digest what's been said, then come back with at least five ways you think you could make sex better for your partner, based on what they've told you. Don't try to put all ten suggestions into the one sex session – you'll end up confused (not to mention exhausted). Instead, consciously try to introduce one new thing each time you make love in the future.

It's a good idea to repeat this exercise a few times during the first year or so. After that, you should be in the habit of talking openly and honestly and able to tell each other what's working and what's not, as it springs to mind.

2. Give each other permission to let loose

When you sleep with someone purely for sex, you can be as wicked as you like because you don't really care what they think of you. Once you fall in love, it's like the censors moved into the bedroom. Will he think I've been around if I suggest that? Will she think I'm kinky if I do this? We switch from being lovers to auditioning as potential Mr and Mrs Rights. Hell, if she could bake a few scones during intercourse, she probably would. The only way to stop the censorship is to talk to each other. Confess your fears, have a laugh about them and reassure each other that there'll be no judging going on.

Each of you has the green light to suggest whatever wild, weird or wonderful activity you'd like.

3. Don't stop masturbating

In fact, do it more. Lots of people think they shouldn't need to masturbate once they're getting regular sex, and if you've just had it 25 times over the weekend you probably *won't* be locking the bathroom door Monday morning. But when your partner's away, they're not in the mood or you just feel extra sexy, masturbating's a great way to keep your libido running hot.

I'd also strongly suggest you take it one step further and do it *in front* of each other. Yup. That's right: a live performance of something you usually do in private. Why? Because partners can't read minds. Body language can speak volumes, talking to each other is essential, but a picture really is worth a thousand words.

Watching each other masturbate, you get to see first-hand what technique you each use – the pressure and speed, how you speed it up or slow it down on approach to orgasm, how you stimulate yourself (or stop) when you're actually having one. All you need to do then is copy each other.

You'd like to try but are too scared to suggest it? If your partner's pretty open about sex, simply start touching yourself the next time you make love. Chances are, they'll sit back and watch, entirely fascinated. If they ignore you or don't notice, say, 'This is how I do it when you're not around,' or, 'I've had fantasies about masturbating in front of you. This feels great.' As you're doing it, get them to put their hand over yours so they can feel the pressure and rhythm you're using. Then remove your hand and let them copy you and give lots of (hopefully positive) feedback.

If you or your partner are a little shy, talk

about it first. Tell them you read a magazine which suggested you can improve your sex life by watching each other masturbate. Follow it up with, 'I'm sure they're right, but as much as I'd like to, I think I'd be too embarrassed.' If they admit they'd also be a little uncomfortable, say, 'This is silly. Why don't we at least try next time?' The more confident partner goes first, prefacing it with something to break the ice ('If you laugh, I'll kill you'). If your lover's really embarrassed, ease them into it. Get them to put their hand on top of yours as you're stimulating them. Once things heat up a little, move your hand out of the way and say, 'Show me, it's easier.' Let them keep their eyes shut if they want: it's *you* that needs to be watching, not them. And, by the way, don't be surprised if you can't orgasm in front of each other when it takes a mere two seconds solo. It's just because you're self-conscious. Persevere though – there are plenty of reasons to give it a try. Watching her masturbate is a popular male fantasy and plenty of women also enjoy the experience. More importantly, it's a guaranteed way to find out how to give your partner an orgasm.

4. Take a guided tour of each other's body

To be the best lover they've ever had, you have to know *all* their hot spots, and this is how you'll find them. Each take turns, but I'll presume here that you're the one doing the exploring first. Get them to lie back, naked and comfortable on the bed. You then use your hands and tongue to explore each part of their body, while they give you a running commentary on how each sensation feels. They don't have to call it like the Grand National – just say, 'Ahh, that feels great,' or, 'That would feel nicer if you did it gentler.' You, of course, are listening and watching intently, discovering what sort of touch turns on what part of their body. One touch won't do for all. Lots of women like their breasts massaged quite firmly, but want a so-gentle-it's-like-a-tickle touch on their clitoris. Start from the top and work downward. And no cheating: skimming straight to the good bits isn't allowed. Slide palms up and down their arms, lick their armpit (both shower first), stroke and kiss their neck, run your fingers through their hair. Move down to the breast area, using fingers, mouth, tongue (maybe even teeth) to find out what they enjoy. Stroke their stomach, down the outside of the thighs, explore behind their knees. Massage feet, suck toes, then slide your palms up their calves and the inside of their thighs. Now – and only now – can you go to work on their genitals. Remember: the idea isn't to make them orgasm, it's a learning exercise. If you feel they're getting too close, switch to a less sensitive area. Once they've climaxed, they won't be half as interested in playing the game.

5. Show him how to stimulate your clitoris

What worked for Jane won't necessarily work for Mary, and it's crucial he gets this bit right for you to orgasm easily. If you did the masturbation exercise, he'll know how to manually stimulate you. But it's dark down there during oral sex and it's also easy for him to lose his bearings during intercourse. So let him have a good look in daylight.

If you're one of the majority of women who can only orgasm during intercourse with extra clitoral stimulation, speak up NOW. Explain it's just the way women are built – a matter of biology rather than penis size or his technique – then, the next time you have intercourse, take his hand and guide him to the spot. Choose positions which allow easy access. It takes more than a few seconds of stroking, so make sure his hand's not twisted or cramped. He should be comfortable while he's doing it so it doesn't detract from his enjoyment. Share the workload: stimulate your clitoris yourself sometimes so he doesn't have to. Or put your hand over his while he's stroking it. You can guide his strokes better and it seems more of a together, two-way thing.

Your libidos don't match

Some people have naturally high sex drives: given the choice between winning Lotto and hot sex every day of their life, they'd kiss the cash goodbye without a moment's hesitation. Sex is as essential to them as oxygen, food and water. Deprived of it, they're like dogs on heat and just as likely to start humping your leg. For others, sex is a pleasant enough experience but not one they'd knock back a nice, hot cup of cocoa for. They enjoy it when it's on offer, but tend to forget about it if it's not. At the bottom of the desire scale are people who are so uninterested or put off by sex, they'd be quite happy if their last legover was their last for life.

In an ideal world, we'd all find our libido equivalents. After all, if you only want to have sex every two months and that suits your partner, it's not a problem. Hook up with a twice-a-day person and it's a huge one. If you find you're a perfect match outside of the bedroom but not in it, this section's for you. It's all about evening up mismatched libidos so you're both a little happier.

They're hot, you're not

You're the one saying, 'Not tonight, honey, I've got a headache'? The first thing I want to say to you is this: it's not your fault. There's a tendency to blame the low-libido person for any sex problems, and that's not fair. Our sex drives are influenced by genes, hormones and past experiences, and not all of it is in your control. Having said that, there *are* ways to kick-start a naturally lazy libido so you'll feel like sex more.

The idea, as always, is to meet your partner in the middle. You boost your desire while they learn to manage theirs (and stop hassling you).

I've aimed this section at both men and women. 'What???!!!' I can hear you splutter. 'A man knocking back sex?' True, it never happens on the soaps – but it does in real life. Men aren't sex robots: they're human, and affected by stress and feelings just as much as women are. Besides, women are demanding little beasts these days and some men find the pressure of having to perform puts them off entirely.

'Whenever I came near her, she'd push me away, even if all I wanted was a cuddle. She made me feel like there was something wrong with me, like I was immature for wanting regular sex. We split and I'm now with a woman who enjoys it as much as I do. I'm marrying this one.'

Aaron, 27, plumber

1. Pinpoint the reason why you don't often feel like sex. It's the obvious place to start. Plenty of people who think they've got naturally low libidos actually haven't. With the right partner, under the right circumstances, they're as randy as the rest of us. So do a bit of soul-searching. Are you simply bored by sex and happy to let other things in life take precedence? Most of us move out of that can't-get-enough stage after a few months. Unfortunately, we replace it with lovemaking that's as predictable as Aunt Martha's gall-bladder operation story. In other words, if steamy, sexy, raunchy sex with George Clooney or Pamela Anderson was on offer, would you be more interested?

Are you tired and physically rundown? Working long hours, staying out too late, too many drinks and ciggies, a diet based around McDonald's – none leave us feeling terribly energetic. Is it temporary disinterest or permanent? At some point, all of us have found the thought of sex about as appealing as filling in a tax return, so think about what else is happening in your life. Are you putting all your energies into something else? If you're trying desperately to score that promotion or working extra hours to pay off the mortgage, there's not much energy left for romping around the bedroom. Stress and tiredness affect our hormones, blocking those that give our libidos a kick, increasing those that make us anxious. (Taking time out, making priorities and planning for sex can solve the problems in a flash.) Are you happy with your body? If you don't feel sexy, it stands to reason you won't feel like it. If you don't like what you see in the mirror, either see a dietician and start exercising or get help if you've got body image problems.

Another biggie: are you in the right relationship? Hooked up with a nice person who does nothing for you below the waist but plenty above? Or trying to force desire for someone who treats you badly? Sex slumps aren't usually just about sex, they're a sign your relationship's gone awry as well. If you have problems outside the bedroom, they leak under the door. Equally as important is your partner's skill as a lover. A bad lover is a common cause of sexual disinterest for women. If he's selfish, inexperienced or incompetent, in other words a bore or boorish in bed, why would you want to initiate a session?

If you've never enjoyed sex, only ever have it because 'you have to' and it rarely satisfies or arouses you, there could be deeper psychological factors at play. An earlier traumatic experience, a strict religious upbringing or growing up being told 'nice girls don't do it' could be responsible, and a visit to a good sex therapist might help. If the thought of sex frightens you or you often feel as if you're 'watching yourself' – you're there but not really there – again, go and see a counsellor.

2. Get back in touch with your sexy side. If it's a temporary lack of desire, consciously concentrate on feelings and sensations when you are having sex, and don't get too hung up on having an orgasm. Start masturbating if you've stopped: the more orgasms you have, the more your body will crave them. Deliberately focus on your erotic self. Read some sexy books, watch erotic movies. Start writing down your favourite fantasies and use them to turn yourself on before sex. Prepare for it mentally. Anticipate what's going to happen. Have a bubble bath instead of a shower and read an erotic book while you're soaking. When you're out with your partner, imagine what that tongue will do to you later. How much better his fingers would feel cupping your breast than wrapped around a beer glass. How she'll look when that sexy little black dress is stripped *off* . . .

3. Make sure you know what turns you on, then tell your partner. Read 'Five steps to a great sex life' on page 136 and work through each. Initially, it'll be an effort. You're not used to giving sex a high priority so you'll need to do it deliberately. Ask yourself regularly: what would I like more of in bed? What would I like less of? Keep a diary and jot down thoughts over a two-week period. Think back to sex you've had in the past that you enjoyed. What was it about it that turned you on? How can you recreate this with your partner? Then pass on what you've discovered. Don't be scared to speak up, to ask for more foreplay or a different oral sex technique. Think outside the square. If you don't feel like intercourse, offer to give your partner oral sex instead. More than one person has changed their mind once they see their partner having such a good time.

4. Learn to receive pleasure. If your problem's long term, you may have grown up feeling guilty about sex and never been 'woken' erotically. In other words, you simply don't know how to respond to sexual sensations in your body. A sensate focus programme is what sex therapists use to help you learn to receive pleasure. This simply involves replacing sex with a series of sensual massages, spaced over a month or so. During the first, you rub oil over your *own* body, to find out what feels good and arouses you. In the next stage, you and your partner massage each other, avoiding the genitals and breasts, reporting back on what feels good and what doesn't. During stage three, you're allowed to touch each other's naughty bits, but still no intercourse. The grand prize at the end is a long overdue, deeply satisfying, good old-fashioned bonk.

5. Ask your partner to be supportive. Explain that you're trying new things to boost your desire but they can help by not pressuring you to have sex when you don't feel like it. Get them to help you relax and feel sexy by reducing the stress level in your life. Sexual desire appears to originate in the brain. If you're juggling so much your brain feels like an amusement park, there aren't too many cells free for fantasy. Ask for some 'pamper time': an hour or two a week when they massage and stroke all the stresses away. (You can return the favour. Just because their libido's not affected, it doesn't mean they won't appreciate a massage.) Ideally, you'd both take a holiday. A few weeks lounging around can revive a lagging libido quicker than *you* can say, 'Let's skip dinner and have sex instead.'

HONEY, WAKE UP! I JUST HAD AN ORGASM

Make no mistake about it. That *was* an orgasm, even if one hand is wrapped around your partner and the other's clutching a teddy bear. It might take ten arduous minutes to masturbate yourself to orgasm in real life, but in your sleep – 'Look, Mum! No hands!'

Around 40 per cent of women experience wet dreams, according to sexologist Alfred Kinsey. It's just more obvious when he's had one (do I really need to explain?). Men have erections once every 90 minutes during the Rapid Eye Movement (REM) stages of sleep, coinciding with the dream period. It now appears women's sexual rhythms mirror those of men: our genitals also become swollen and lubricated. For some women, night-time orgasms are the only ones they'll have. British sex expert Anne Hooper says she's encountered women who could orgasm ➤

in their sleep, but couldn't through masturbation or with a partner. Why? It's the old cliché – the brain is the ultimate sex organ, and when we're asleep any emotional blocks (like sexual hang-ups) are removed.

According to Hooper, we're more likely to have a wet dream when we're not having regular sex. If we're single, our partner's away or been too busy with work to indulge, wet dreams are a wake-up call: you're not getting enough in real life. They can also be the result of having unsatisfying sex with a partner before falling asleep. Your body, very politely, finishes the job for you.

If you can remember the content of a dream that resulted in a bonus orgasm, pay attention. Force yourself to wake up and write down everything you can remember: where was it, what were they doing, how were they doing it, what were you feeling? When we dream, our subconscious allows us to fantasize guilt-free: you'll come up with scenarios you'd blush at if you'd daydreamed ➤

them. Often, it's your subconscious desires tapping you on the shoulder, saying, 'Hey, boring, be a bit more adventurous will you?' You dreamed of making love outdoors? Introduce some alfresco sex into your real life. Being seduced forcefully? Play out a slave–master fantasy. The only thing you *shouldn't* pay too much attention to is *who* you were having sex with in the dream. Dreaming of sex with a member of your family or of someone the same sex as you, for instance, doesn't mean you've got secret incestuous desires or gay tendencies. It's more to do with what they represent. If you adore your brother, he could simply represent sex with someone you feel comfortable with as opposed to a partner you're uptight about. If you're in bed with someone of the same sex, it's sometimes a narcissistic dream: you're actually making love to yourself. So don't get too hung up on the weird, freaky elements – concentrate on the yummy nice bits.

You're hot, they're *not*

'Is that all you ever think about?' 'Stop mauling me!' 'I get it, you're pissed off because you didn't get it this morning, aren't you!' Just as your partner's feeling the pressure of not wanting sex enough, you're getting a battering for wanting it too much. And since we always want what we can't have, constantly being knocked back only seems to fuel your desire more. What to do?

1. Take matters into your own hands – literally. Masturbate often to take the edge off. And drop the 'why should I have to when I'm in a relationship?' attitude. Your partner's not there to service you, it's not their *job* to keep you sexually satisfied. You're together because you love each other and want to make each other happy. Constantly hassling them for sex does the opposite. Masturbate every second time you feel like sex. Ideally, you'd tell your partner what you're up to so you don't have to lock yourself away, but make sure you don't make them feel guilty. There's a difference between stomping off ('I suppose I'll have to do it by myself – again') and giving a wink as you head for the bathroom with a sexy mag ('Be back in a minute, sweetheart. Get ready for a cuddle'). Even better, get into the habit of doing it in front of them. Your partner might be more than happy to watch you pleasure yourself, even if they aren't in the mood for sex themselves.

2. Don't force your partner to have sex. Stop putting pressure on someone to have sex and you'll give them time to actually feel like it. That doesn't mean you can't be affectionate or sensual, just make it clear when you *are* innocently kissing or touching your partner that there's no hidden agenda. You should be able to snuggle up on the couch and watch a video together without immediately suctioning your hands to her breasts. Ditto his penis. Stick to stroking arms, shoulders and neck and you'll ignite desire rather than quash it.

3. When you do make love, focus on their pleasure, not yours. The better lover you are and the more enjoyment they get from sex, the more likely they are to crave it. Encourage them to open up and tell you what they need to get turned on. Do you need to brush up on your technique? Do they need more foreplay? Are you picking the wrong time for sex (like Saturday mornings, the only chance they get to sleep in)? Suggest you take a bath together or give them a massage first. Ask for feedback during sex and above all, give them *time* to get aroused. Lower-libido people often take a little longer. Just because your genitals can spring to attention while reading about cross-pollination in *Green Foliage: A Guide*, doesn't mean their arousal system is permanently on automatic.

Help! My partner's awful in bed

You're crazy about them but think you really will go mad if you have to put up with ho-hum sex for the rest of your life? Take heart – and take action by trying the following.

Pick your time to talk

Make sure it's out of the bedroom. The absolute worst thing to do is erupt into a frustrated, fiery stream of criticisms while the bedsprings are still bouncing. Wait until

'For years, I put up with truly awful sex. It was like being served up broccoli and peas for dinner every night when you hate the stuff. Eventually, I plucked up the courage to tell him I wasn't happy. Predictably, he stormed out. But he came back in an hour and said, "Okay, let me have it." We talked for hours and haven't stopped. I'm happy and he's enjoying sex so much more as well.'

Fiona, 39, journalist

you're both comfortable, happy and chatting freely. Then say, 'Darling, I really love our relationship and adore making love with you. Is there anything you'd like me to do in bed that I'm not already? There's so many things we can explore together.' It's less threatening to kick off the chat by talking about new things you'd both like to try, *then* you can gently work it around to how satisfied each of you are. If they're not terribly forthcoming on this point, you go first to give them an idea of how to word things. 'When I give you oral sex, I never know whether to keep going while you're climaxing or stop?' Most people are polite enough to then ask, 'What about you? Are you happy?' If they don't, turn it around yourself by saying, 'I love it when you ——. Can you do it more often?'

Concentrate on what they're doing right

Saying, 'Harold, if you keep on doing that weird thing with your tongue I'll go completely nuts,' won't get you very far. Saying, 'Honey, it feels fabulous when you do X, but it would feel even better if you moved a little to the left/did it for longer,' will. Even if your partner truly is pathetic, there must be something nice you can say about them. Even if it's, 'It turns me on so much watching your muscles flex when you're on top of me.'

Let your body talk

The next time you have sex, use body language to show what you do and don't like and you'll get the point across far more effectively. When they do something you like or they're on the right track, exaggerate your response: moan loudly, move closer, kiss them harder so they can't help but get the message you like what they're doing. If you don't like something, make that obvious as well. Twist away, lift your body away from their touch or (better still) redirect their hand or mouth or whatever. Most people do to their partners what they'd like done to them. If you like having your neck kissed or bitten, kiss and bite theirs. If they don't get the hint, say, 'Do you like that? I love it, too.' Remember to ask, not order. Boss them around with, 'Do this, do that,' and they'll feel resentful. Besides, it's about as satisfying as asking someone to tell you they love you.

You thought everything was fixed but they seem to have forgotten all you've said three sessions on? It's very easy to get carried away in the heat of the moment and forget your partner needs their left toe sucked at the crucial moment. If this happens, just remind them. Whisper in their ear, 'Honey, remember you said you'd ——'

LOVE BITES . . .

Men are able to recite, in detail, what they do once they're in the bedroom, but it's women who remember each and every step in the flirtation game that got them there.

❗ As much as we don't like to admit it, women are turned on by porn almost as much as he is. Our testosterone level shoots up by 80 per cent when watching a flesh flick. His goes up by 100 per cent.

❗ Would you sleep with the boss to keep your job? More than two-fifths of men would. Forty-two per cent said they'd bed a female superior if forced to choose between sex and redundancy. But she has to be attractive. Half would reconsider if she wasn't dishy.

❗ SEX – that's what 50 per cent of men said when asked their favourite thing to do in bed.
READ – that's what 75 per cent of women answered when asked the same question.

Men with symmetrical features give their partners more orgasms but they're also more likely to be unfaithful. Why? They're more attractive to women, so have had more practice, but they're also spoilt for choice.

Dish up desire . . . Fresh figs followed by sausages? Baby potatoes artfully arranged around a whole baked courgette? Not exactly a gourmet's delight but if it's *after*-dinner activity you're after, these are the meals to serve. According to 'the law of similarities', foods that resemble sexual organs give us a subconscious jolt in all the right places. Banana Split anyone?

Sixty-two per cent of men and 73 per cent of women say they find their partners more sexually attractive now than when they first met.

5

Sex Troubleshooting: The 8 most-asked couple questions
....

Ⓜ **Why doesn't she initiate sex more?**

It could be because you jump in before she's had a chance to make the first move herself. Or maybe it's because she's worried she'll come across as 'unladylike'.

When I was at uni, every psychology student had to 'volunteer' to participate in a number of psychology experiments in order to pass the course. For one, we were all seated in a class-room, arranged in boy–girl format, then presented with large, blank notepads and a pen. The professor beamed down at us from his lectern and asked, terribly politely, for us to write down all the slang words we'd ever heard used to describe the male and female genitals.

Now, at 20, all of us knew plenty. The guys scribbled ferociously, constantly checking the competition in a bid to be the last in the room to stop writing. The more he knew, the more sexually experienced he'd seem. The girls did the opposite. Twirling our hair and gazing innocently out of the window for supposed inspiration, we made the odd pathetic scribble, then crossed out whatever it was we'd written. After eavesdropping on my big brother for years, I could have filled the entire notebook. Sue, queen of dirty jokes, could have filled six of them but even she feigned disinterest and a complete lack of knowledge. Why? Because it wasn't done for females to be seen as too in touch with the raw, primitive side of sex. None of us could bear being thought of as a 'slut' by filling the page.

That's what may be at the bottom of your girlfriend's reluctance to initiate sex. If she grew up in a religious, strict household, I'd bet that is at the root of the problem. Tell her you'd love it if she was the one to make the first move and see how she reacts. If she opens up and confesses she's worried about being judged, reassure her profusely. You could also try buying her some erotic fiction, written by a female (try Anaïs Nin as well as modern writers), so she'll get the message it's okay these days for women to feel and be sexy. Incidentally, you're not alone in wanting her to initiate sex more often. Relationships expert Dr Maryon Tysoe cites a US study where psychologists asked dating or newly married couples what they'd like more of in bed. Men, much more than women, wanted their partners to have more experimental sex, spontaneous sex, initiate sex more often and play the dominant role.

Ⓜ Ⓕ **When I was single, I was desperate for regular sex. Now it's on tap, I've gone off it. Why?**

It's a bit like Christmas. You can smell that turkey cooking and you're practically *drooling*. Come the day after Boxing Day, you'd rather eat mashed-up grasshoppers than face another slice. You really *can* have too much of a good thing. Most couples gorge themselves on each other's bodies when they first get together. They're overfull, then keep topping up.

When you're single, sex isn't always available so that's all you think about. We want what we can't have. When you live with someone, you can have sex whenever you damn well please. Add to that, *he's* (I'm not being sexist but it is usually the guy) almost always ready, willing and able for sex, and you start to see why desire can wane. At first, being woken up by hands on your breasts and an erect penis sticking in your back is sexy. You think, 'Brilliant! Regular sex again.' Six weeks in, it's like, 'Oh for God's sake. Does that thing ever go down? Get *off* me!'

If your partner *always* wants sex, you never get time to build an appetite for it.

'I never, ever get the chance to initiate sex because Mark's always suggested it before I have the chance to *think* a sexy thought, let alone carry it through,' says a girlfriend of mine. 'We never go without it, so I never have time to miss it.'

If you never get the chance to reach out first, if you're always asked before getting an opportunity to do the asking, your sexual feelings wither. You start to feel pressured and used and lose interest altogether.

'I was totally bored with our sex life until my

boyfriend lost interest because he was working so hard,' says Annette. 'After a week of him falling straight to sleep instead of hassling me for a bit, I suddenly realized I missed sex and started kissing him hard.

He said, 'Sweetheart, I'm too tired,' which fired me up even more. Suddenly, I *desperately* wanted sex and did stuff I'd never do normally in an attempt to turn him on. Not only did it make me realize how it feels on his end, I've never felt sexier because it was me wanting sex first. I was the seductress and he was the seduced – and he loved it. Now we play this game where he pretends to feign sleep and I have to wake him up . . .'

F   **My boyfriend wants me to do kinky things in bed. I'm not sure.**

'Kinky' is a very subjective term because what's kinky to one is standard sexual behaviour for another. So you need to establish whether what your boyfriend's suggesting is worth trying once (and you're being a little uptight) or if it's way out there and best left as a fantasy. If you can't check with a good friend, look up a sex book. Is it listed as something most couples give a whirl now and again or under deviant behaviours? If it's under 'deviant' or includes other people, I'd be wary. Ditto if it involves physical pain (and just a quick word on anal sex: if you're going to try it, read a good sex book first. There's a right and wrong way to approach it).

If his request seems reasonable, look at your attitude to sex generally. Think back to any comments past lovers have made and conversations you've had about sex with your girlfriends. Do they seem much more laidback about it than you are? Far more sexually adventurous? Maybe it's time to push yourself out of your comfort zone. If your relationship with your boyfriend is good, you trust him and know he'd stop if you didn't like it, why not try it once and see how you feel?

If you decide not to give it a go, come up with something else new that appeals to both of you. That way he won't feel cheated and you're working together to keep sex fresh and exciting (which is, of course, why he wants to try something different in the first place).

Ⓜ Ⓕ I suspect all my partner wants from me is sex, even though we've been going out a few months. How do I find out for sure and let them know I want more than that?

Do they only want to see you when they're positive sex is on the agenda? Are they only interested in you when you're naked? Is 'Your place or mine' the only whole sentence they utter? Then, they're only in it for the sex. But if they're simply ravishing you as often as possible, it could be they're stuck at the shagarama stage of your relationship while you're ready to move onto the lovey-dovey bit. Why not suggest a few dates that obviously won't end up in the bedroom: a picnic in a public place, going shopping together or seeing a movie (all minus the detours back home). If they refuse or grumble, ask them outright what the story is. Can they see a future between you or is it purely no-strings sex? If they say it's more than that, ask if they'd like to make the relationship monogamous. It's a fair question after a few months and guaranteed to have them sweating if they're not in it for the long haul.

M F **We've got a motto in our office that sex in another country doesn't count. In other words, if there's absolutely no way your partner will find out, what's wrong with it?**

Here's a true story that'll chill you to the bone: a girlfriend of mine had a three-night fling during a work trip to LA. About six months later, she got a call at work to say a 'surprise' visitor was waiting for her in reception.

'Hi!' her LA lover said. 'I remembered where you worked and thought I'd drop in.'

Jesus! she thought and quickly shuffled him off into a corner.

Thinking she was being intimate, he squeezed her bottom and grinned wickedly, 'Any chance of a very long lunch? I haven't stopped thinking about your body since the conference. God, the sex was good!'

From behind her a very familiar voice said, 'I

think it's all over, Cassandra.' Her boyfriend had walked through the door that very second to see if she wanted to grab a coffee. Three-year relationship over.

Quite apart from surprise visits, sleeping with someone else counts as betrayal, whether you do it at home or overseas. Yes, it's tempting. Yes, lots of people do give in under those circumstances and if you're determined to do it, there's a lot *less* risk of being caught. But it's *never* guaranteed you won't be. Weigh up if you're prepared to lose what you have at home and if the answer's no, don't do it.

Ⓜ Ⓕ My partner wants me to talk dirty to him during sex. I've got no real objections to it but don't know quite what to say.

Years ago, the same thing happened to me. The mood was hot and heavy, we were in the middle of a passionate kiss when suddenly my boyfriend said, 'Talk dirty to me.' I looked at him blankly. Like you, I didn't have any objections but all I could think to say was, 'Give it to me, big boy,' and I sure as hell couldn't say that without laughing. It is hard not to come across like a poorly paid extra from a porn film.

It's probably best to tackle it this way. Start by simply making noise during sex – groan, moan, say, 'Ummmmm.' The next time, try, 'God, that feels so nice,' or, 'I can't tell you what this is doing to me.' Once you've broken the silence, the rest is easy. Try giving him a running commentary of every sexy thought that's going through your head: how much of a turn-on this or that is, how you get hot by being able to make him excited, what you'd like him to do to you, what you're going to do to him . . .

Use fantasy as a springboard. Say you had a sexy dream last night (make one up), then tell him about it while you're having sex. The more detailed and explicit the better, but even, 'You took my clothes off and we made love on a beach,' is better than nothing. Match the pace of the dream or fantasy to your love-making. As the fantasy climaxes, so do you.

He wants you to use four-letter words? Even if you're the type that only says 'gosh' outside the bedroom, would it really kill you to let loose in it? Being 'naughty' by using language you wouldn't dream of usually is all part of the fun and the turn-on. It's also a healthy way to exorcise the good-girls-don't-enjoy-sex hang-up and he'll love seeing your wanton side.

(F) **I adore my boyfriend of two years but can't stop fantasizing about sex with his friends and other guys. Does this mean I've fallen out of love with him?**

No – though it could mean you're a tad bored with your sex life. What's more likely is that you've simply got a healthily high libido and a vivid imagination. People often feel guilty if they fantasize about someone else while making love to their partner, but it's more common than you think and, in my view, totally acceptable. I wouldn't tell or even hint to your boyfriend you're mentally lusting after his friends, but it's a far cry from being unfaithful in reality. Fantasies are a way to add spice and variety without the moral dilemmas and complications of an affair. Indulge guilt-free.

Ⓜ **I seem to want and enjoy sex much more than my girlfriend. How can I get her to the same level?**

Stop blaming. Don't persecute her for being the less 'sexy' partner. You don't enjoy being accused of being a 'sex maniac'.

Be honest with each other. Work out how often you'd like to make love per fortnight. Ask her to do the same, then compromise. If you say three times and she says six, settle on four one week, five the next.

Make sex as good as possible. Sorry to keep harping on it but if I get nothing else through, I'm determined you'll remember this: the more you enjoy sex, the more you'll want to do it. If her libido isn't as high as yours, it's in your interest to make sex so bloody fantastic, you override her 'natural' urge.

Keep her healthy. Make sure she gets enough sleep, exercise, eats healthily. The better she feels physically, the more energy she'll have for sex.

LOVE BITES . . .

It's official: no-one likes an overtly jealous partner but most have a touch of the green-eyed monster themselves. When researchers surveyed 6,800 people in 20 different countries, they found:

· Eighty-three per cent of people believe jealousy can ruin even the best relationships – though 49 per cent found 'mild' jealousy flattering.

· Forty-nine per cent would never stay with a jealous partner – but only 39 per cent trust their partners implicitly and wouldn't check up on them.

· The most jealous people live in Turkey and Spain, though 90 per cent of Portuguese spy on their lovers.

· What if you never get jealous? Fifty-four per cent of those surveyed say you're not in love!

What's the perfect position to talk intimately with your partner? About five feet away from each other, sitting face to face. Women are uncomfortable discussing personal matters from further away; men don't like it when women

*move closer. Five feet is the happy
medium.*

So much for male bonding. One in five
men would make a pass at his best
friend's girlfriend. But only one in 30 women
said they'd do the same.

Myth: Women nag more than men do.
Reality: It's true. And we do it twice as
often. Researchers say it's because women
have got more to complain about, especially
if we're married. Even if you both work, it's
still usually the wife who's saddled with
most of the domestics (and the kids). He
doesn't nag because he's got little to gripe
about!

Turn on the stereo to turn on each other.
When researchers asked men and women
worldwide, 'What gives you the most

pleasure in life?' the majority said listening to music. Sex came a close second. For the ultimate pleasure experience? Bop while you bonk.

6

And if it all goes Horribly Wrong . . .

THE GET-OVER-IT GUIDE: DAY BY DAY, STEP BY STEP TO MENDING A BROKEN HEART (AND WHY IT'S NEVER EASY)

You knew it was coming. But hearing them say, 'It's over,' and imagining it are two totally different things. In your fantasy, they take both your hands in theirs and deliver the tragic news in a voice cracked with emotion. Invariably, they're leaving for a reason that has nothing to do with you (the army needs them, they've decided to devote their life to God). You nod quietly, delivering one, hauntingly touching parting line ('Go – but you take my heart with you'). They head for the door then stop dead as they hear you catch a sob. Their back still turned to you, one hand on the doorknob, they say (struggling for composure): 'I have to do this. I can't ask you to wait for me but . . .'

Reality is somewhat different. You both sit awkwardly on the couch because you know what's coming. 'It's just not working,' they blurt out. 'FINE!' you say. 'That's just BLOODY WONDERFUL!' Then you start screaming, 'You CAN'T *LEEEEEAVE* ME!' fall in a pathetic heap at their feet, wrap both arms around their legs and burst into a hysterical sobbing fit punctuated with unattractive hiccups and snorts. They start to head for the door, you're forced to endure the indignity of being dragged across the carpet because you won't let go of their legs. Desperate to get away, they kick you free and sprint for the door, slamming it behind them. You're after them quick smart, throwing yourself and anything else you can get your hands on in their general direction. Their parting words aren't 'Wait for me', but 'Get away from me, you psychopath!' You follow with a supremely clever 'Get stuffed, you bastard/ bitch! I hate you!'

Then the anger goes and you go back inside, slide down the wall, hit the floor and give in to total panic. You're crying so much you can't breathe. You feel dizzy, think you're going to be sick and are, right there on the carpet. Stumbling toward the bathroom, you visualize the packet of razor blades in the cabinet and sensibly do a detour to the kitchen in search of vodka. One swig and you're sick again. You think, *This is what dying must feel like.* Because that's exactly how you do feel: dead. What's the point of life if they're not going to be there to share it with you?

Getting through the next 30 seconds seems impossible when someone's put your heart through a mincer. But you *will* get through the next minute and the next hour and the next day and the next year. However painful it is now, *you will survive*. How do I know? Because I've been there, everyone I know has been there, and I'd bet money on it that you could fit all the people who *haven't* been there into one small, sad little room. You loved, you lost – but at least you loved. We all came out the other side – so will you. Clear the tears long enough to stop the page blurring and I'll tell you how it's done.

How to use the get-over-it guide

I admit it. The time frame of this guide is ridiculously optimistic, deliberately so. It's not just designed to give you practical advice on how to get through, it's designed to give you hope. The time frames I've organized it under are probably irrelevant, anyway, because every split-up is different and every person heals at a different rate. But most of you will go through all the different stages, usually in this order:

- **Stage 1:** the intensely painful bit. This can last anywhere from two weeks to two months, depending on your relationship. Getting through each day is difficult and you think you'll never be happy again.

- **Stage 2:** is spent adjusting to being single again. It might take a month to six months to stop yourself saying and thinking 'X and I', and come to terms with being 'one'.

- **Stage 3:** is when you start truly healing. If you went out for a year or so and thought it was forever, this will probably happen about six months after the split. If it was longer, it could take up to a year. You feel normal most of the time but are still battling memories or analysing what went wrong every week or few weeks.

- **Stage 4:** you made it! Official recovery can take anywhere from one to two years.

Don't panic if you appear to move onto the next stage, then slip back one for a few weeks – it's normal. But that's what you're in for. Hopefully, the following guide will help get you from one to four in record time!

Week one

F FOR HER: THE DAY IT HAPPENS

Get on the phone as quickly as possible, the minute he walks out of the door. Call your closest friend, your Mum, big brother, the *butcher*, if you have a special bond: anyone who will understand. Ask them to come over immediately, stopping only for supplies (tissues, alcohol, chocolate, poison to drop into his drink next time he's out). While they're hot-footing it to your house (allow time for speeding tickets), call another friend and let,

'Oh, poor darling,' and, 'I always knew he'd hurt you,' drone on in the background while you hiccup and create a mini tidal wave of tears on the floor. Don't put the receiver down until the doorbell rings, then (and only then) you're allowed to lose it completely. Cry, beat the wall, cling onto your friend for dear life but let out as much grief as possible. When you feel remotely calm, sit down, have a drink and pour out the whole sad, sorry tale over and over until they not only know what happened, they're living it with you. He said, then I said . . . Did I tell you he said then I said? Keep going until you can't analyse it any further or your friend falls asleep. If they can't stay with you, let them bundle you up and take you to their house. Tonight is not the night to be alone.

Ⓜ FOR HIM: THE DAY IT HAPPENS

Initially, you're in shock. You keep thinking, *She'll get over it. Any minute now, she'll call me to say sorry and everything will be fine*. You consider sending flowers – that's worked before. Except you know this is different. She doesn't call, and when you call her four hours later, she says, ever-so-gently, 'I meant it. I'm sorry. It really is over.'

If you can do it (yes, you can), let yourself have a good cry. When you're done, pick up the phone and call someone. If you've got a close female friend, she's first on the list. Tell her your girlfriend's left you and you're feeling down. Could she come over and cheer you up? She'll be over at your place in a nanosecond, dispensing hugs and all sorts of soothing there-theres (and no, she won't tell everyone how pathetic you were, so drop the macho act). No close female friends? Call a mate. He'll drag you down to the local pub for a game of pool, give you a slap on the back and say, 'You'll get over it – I did.' It's not much, but it is true. Whatever you end up doing, tonight is not the night to start the Liver Cleansing Diet. If a few beers make you feel better, have them but keep it under control. The idea is to send you to sleep – not stumbling over to her house drunk.

Ⓜ Ⓕ BOTH CLING TO THIS

Think back to when you helped someone get over a painful break-up. Remember how they said they'd never smile again, but you knew they'd get over it? They did – and so will you.

Day two

Ⓕ FOR HER

The first thing you realize when you open your eyes the next day is that you can't: they're swollen shut from so much crying. Reality starts to seep through when you get out of bed and stand on a mound of crumpled tissues. Instant tears. It hits with full force: he's gone, you're alone. Day two (sorry) is even worse than day one, so aim to simply get through it.

It's a weekend

Spend the day repeating the story (for the 45th time) to a friend, any friend. You'll feel raw, miserable and so sorry for yourself it's not funny, so surround yourself with people who care. True friends will let you tag along wherever they go: take them up on it. If they're cleaning the loo, hand them the loo cleaner; if they're shaving their legs, the razor (actually, maybe you'd better skip that one). It's wallow-in-it day, so don't feel guilty about dominating the conversation totally and not having cleaned your teeth for 24 hours. The only no-no today: DON'T call him and don't persuade your friends to call him either. Resist the urge to park outside his house, do a drive-by *or* turn up at his best friend's hoping for some inside info. Make a pact with yourself that you can call him in one week if you still need to and get a friend to help you stick to it. (The deal: you have to call them before you call him.)

It's a work day

Get up, put your make-up on and get out that door. You'll be tempted to call in sick and pull the bedclothes over your head, but you're not doing yourself any favours. If you feel so traumatized you honestly can't make it, call in sick, but get yourself to a friend's house – don't stay at home alone. You've dragged yourself into the office? Great – but it's unlikely you'll be Ms Efficient, so tell your immediate boss what's happened. You know you won't perform well, but would prefer to be there and you'll make up for lost time later and so on. If you're on friendly terms with your workmates, let them know you're hurting (and accept all offers of lunch, cream cakes and cups of hot, sweet tea).

If it's a brisk, professional team and you don't

feel comfortable blabbing all, put on a brave front and make calls to friends and family in your lunch hour. If you can't hold it together, disappear into the toilet and take your make-up bag to do a quick repair job. Call a friend to see for dinner tonight: their place or yours. If you can't face sleeping alone, crash in front of the telly with the sound turned *up*.

Ⓜ FOR HIM

Read the 'For her' section because you'll feel exactly the same. If you picked up the phone and someone said, 'Congratulations, you've just won the lottery!' your first thought would be, *I wonder if a million dollars would change her mind?* Fill up your day with activity. Play sport, watch reruns of old sitcoms, strip the car engine then put it back together again: anything to keep yourself busy and keep your mind off it.

It's the weekend

Get on the phone and don't get off it until you've organized non-stop entertainment for the entire weekend. Tell people you've split up, even if you do play it cool and insist you don't care (they'll make their own conclusions). If you don't want to talk about it, tell people. Say, 'It's over. I don't want to talk about it. I'll tell you the details later.' People will want to spoil you: let them. It's not being 'weak' to accept offers of roast dinners, it's what friends do. Your main aim today: convincing yourself that turning up at her front door with enough red roses to fill her entire flat really won't work. If she's serious about splitting, she'll just feel sorry for you.

It's a work day

You're one up on your female equivalent: chances are you'll get through the day without dissolving into tears. If you think you can get through on autopilot, do it. If you can't, tell your boss what's happened. If possible, arrange to meet a friend for lunch, but steer clear of the nearest pub. I don't care how fabulous she was or how bad you feel, she's not worth losing your job over by going back to work drunk.

Ⓜ Ⓕ BOTH CLING TO THIS

Before you finally go to sleep, tell yourself, 'I'm okay. I'm just upset. I will get through this. I survived today didn't I?'

Day three
Ⓜ Ⓕ FOR HIM AND HER

Okay, enough of this namby-pamby wimpy stuff: today is toughen-up day. I'm being cruel? Humour me, anyway, and give it a go. You've got nothing to lose except a day feeling powerless. Today it's time for some action: I want you to gather up all those relationship reminders and put them out of sight. That's right: books, cards, letters, photographs, CDs with your song on them, cute little notes, anything at all which connects them to you. If Special Frosty Pops brings back memories, plonk it in the bin. (If *everything* does, perhaps you'd better wait a week.) Put all that memorabilia into a big bag and either throw it all out (best), give it to a friend to look after (okay) or shove it in the back of a cupboard where you can't get to it without a huge effort (a cop-out, but better than leaving it in sight).

Wash the sheets and towels (yes, you must), then go through your diary and cancel any events where you're bound to run into each other. Stay away from all your old haunts: the secluded beach you both discovered, the great little Thai restaurant that was your favourite. Avoid anything that reminds you of your ex. Why? Because you really are kidding yourself if you think lying around listening to 'your song' and rereading old love letters is going to help you heal or magically get them back. It won't. In fact, if there honestly *is* any hope of a reconciliation, seeing you get on with your life is far more likely to do it. It's been proven over and over: act like you don't need them (even if you do want them) and they may well realize they want you too.

So if they come over to beg forgiveness and notice their picture's been removed, you'll win respect not disapproval. *The quicker you accept they're gone for good – even if they aren't – the quicker you'll get over them, and the more likely it is they'll want to return.* It's a win–win situation. You're not only upping the chances of getting back together, you're upping your chances of happily getting on with your life if they don't. The reverse is also true: send letters begging another chance, pester them with phone calls, follow them around and they'll thank God they got out when they did. Besides, your ego's been bruised enough, it can't take any more knocks right now, so don't set your-self up for them.

Ⓜ Ⓕ BOTH CLING TO THIS

There are whole minutes – perhaps even two or three together – that you don't think about your ex. You are recovering.

Day four

Ⓕ FOR HER

From now on, you're only allowed five minutes crying time a day. Yup. It sounds bizarre but I want you to try really hard to hold it all in until you're allowed to let it all out. Schedule a time and once the floodgates open, set the timer because in five minutes you have to stop and reward yourself. Follow every crying session with something that makes you feel good. Slap on a face mask, some empowering music (Alanis Morrisette, 'Jagged Little Pill', The Corrs, 'I

Never Loved You Anyway') on the CD player and soak in a bubble bath with your favourite mag. If you're reading this and thinking, *I can't stop crying for five minutes, let alone restrict it to that*, you're officially allowed to move this step back a little. (And if you're feeling seriously out of control, get yourself an emergency appointment with a good counsellor.)

Ⓜ FOR HIM

If you're a typical bloke, you probably haven't spoken too much about how you're feeling. Now's a good time to call that female friend and pour it all out to her. If you don't have one, or feel uncomfortable talking about your feelings, write it all down. Get yourself a beer (or coffee) and take an hour or so to write down everything you're feeling and going through. No-one's going to see it (burn it afterward, if you're paranoid), so be totally honest. Record how you seriously thought she was the one, the plans you had, how you started reading the fine print at the bottom of the diamond ads. What you miss about her, how she made you feel ten feet tall and now you feel about one inch high. Why you think you broke up, how you'll never, ever trust anyone ever again or fall in love. Ever.

Yes, it sounds pathetic and you'll feel pathetic as you're writing it all down. But it truly will help. So just keep writing and let it all come out. You'll cry a lot and feel exhausted when you've finished but at least you've released some of the pain and it's not festering inside. Face your emotions *now*, feel the pain *now* and you'll give yourself a chance to recover. If you push them to some dark place deep inside you, you risk them resurfacing when you next meet someone you really like. It's hard enough making new relationships work without having to grapple with all the old stuff Jayne left behind at the same time.

Ⓜ Ⓕ FOR BOTH OF YOU

Keep as busy as possible and *don't sit by the phone*. Let's be logical here: if the former love of your life suddenly decides they want to live forever in your pocket, they're not going to give up if you're not home when they ring. If they do, it was a spur-of-the-moment (they didn't pull last night) thing. Or they're simply calling to see how you are. Don't return the call or pick up the phone if you're pretty sure that's all they want. Talking with them will send you straight back to longing-for-them land. Call a friend and ask them to relay a message: you're hurting but you're okay and don't want to hear from them for a little while.

By day four you're still utterly miserable – though more in a depressed than out-of-control way. Nevertheless, keep surrounding yourself with understanding friends and protect your heart. If a soppy song comes on the radio, switch stations. Ditch any novel that has love scenes for gutsy thrillers, choose your movies very carefully and buy some party music to replace those banned CDs.

Ⓜ Ⓕ BOTH CLING TO THIS

All this heartache has made you remember how bloody awful you felt when you split with another ex. You got over them – maybe, just maybe, you'll survive this one too.

Day five

Ⓜ Ⓕ FOR BOTH OF YOU

Today you officially take back control of your life by doing some spring-cleaning. If it's a work day, start with your office. Spend your lunch hour going through every single 'to do' pile and organizing it properly. Clear out your drawers, ruthlessly throw out everything you don't need or file it where it belongs.

When you get home that evening, turn the CD player up full blast (happy music, not sad stuff) and do the same at home. Empty all the cupboards and throw out or donate anything useless or stuff you haven't worn or used in the last two years. Rearrange the furniture. Make a list of things to buy that'll brighten up the place. You've just started on the kitchen and it's midnight already? Who cares? You're not sleeping that well anyway – you might as well completely exhaust yourself and have something to show for it in the morning other than knotted sheets. Tomorrow you'll wake up to a clean, organized flat and office and feel a sense of satisfaction.

Ⓜ Ⓕ BOTH CLING TO THIS

Believe in fate. Everything happens for a reason. Perhaps you broke up with your ex because someone even better is out there waiting for you or you're about to get that promotion and need all your energy for work. Trust in your future.

Day six

M **F** FOR BOTH OF YOU

Okay, you're still down and feeling terrible but after five or six days should have a little perspective on the situation. You did some physical spring-cleaning yesterday; today we're going to do some emotional spring-cleaning. If you're a guy (and did as you were told), you will have already written down all the emotions you're experiencing. If you're female, you've no doubt verbalized them to your friends. This list is different.

The best strategy to accept someone is gone is to collect as much evidence as possible to prove a) you're a wonderful person who deserves better, and b) they weren't as fabulous as you thought. I'm not being nasty or vengeful, just realistic. After all, if they were *that* perfect for you, they wouldn't have dumped you in the first place. There were obviously areas where you didn't see eye to eye and things you didn't like about them. They were human, weren't they?

Start with list number one: get a good friend to help you write down everything great about yourself, all your successes and achievements. You're a great friend. Popular. A terrific listener. Your family adore you. You were crucial in helping your team win the final. You can sink 12 beers and still stand. Write down big achievements, serious things, silly things – as many as you can come up with.

List two: set to work on your ex. It doesn't matter how much you did or do love them, no-one is perfect (not even them). Write down every single flaw and weakness you can think of. How they didn't share your passion for the sea, how your Mum never really liked them, the time you caught them admiring themselves in the mirror, how they flirted at parties, the embarrassing green trackpants that made their bum look six times bigger, how they'd give you a hard time for wanting to watch 'crap', how he vomited all over the bathroom floor after a night with the boys, how she used to leave little hairs from shaving all over the bath.

Every time a friend calls, ask them to help you add to the list – but make sure you explain your motives. Friends will be suspicious if you ask them to bag the person, because they're worried you'll use it against them if the two of you get back together. Explain that it's a silly little exercise you want to do to support you right now, and you'll be amazed what nasties they'll come up with!

Ⓜ Ⓕ BOTH CLING TO THIS

Look at yourself in the mirror every morning and evening and say to yourself, 'It's over. They're not coming back. I will survive.' Keep on doing this until you can look yourself straight in the eyes, speak confidently and believe it.

Day seven
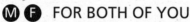 FOR BOTH OF YOU

Get out your diary and phone book and spend the day calling all the people you've neglected during your relationship. Prepare what you're going to say when they ask about your ex (a simple, 'It didn't work out,' is fine). Make dates with everyone until your diary looks satisfyingly full. Give opposite-sex friends preference: they'll give you the ego boost you need, but be careful with exes. It's extremely tempting to convince yourself they really were 'the one' when you're feeling vulnerable and lonely. (They weren't.)

I wouldn't accept invitations to go out and party just yet – you're still too raw. Instead, plan evenings with good friends and happy couples. No, you won't look at them and feel envious – you'll see living evidence of people who've been through what you're going through and had the courage to fall in love again. Ask them (separately) to recount the details of their past break-ups. How they never thought they'd love again but here they are, doing just that.

Ⓜ Ⓕ BOTH CLING TO THIS

Do I honestly believe I'm not going to meet anyone else in the next ten years?

Week two

Congratulations! Here you were thinking you couldn't make it through a minute and you survived an entire week without a) joining the French Foreign Legion; b) joining a cult; or c) moving back to the country to live with Mum. A shred of self-respect should be resurfacing.

By now, you're probably making about three 'God, I feel awful' calls to friends a day and are able to spend half an hour on your own without feeling suicidal. Now's the time to cut the umbilical cord completely. Ask mutual friends not to report back every piece of gossip about your ex – and vice versa. Don't spend your life trying to find out about theirs. If they're depressed, it'll give you false hope. They're out dancing until dawn – your ego will take another dive.

Beware of friends who encourage you to believe your ex will 'wake up to themselves' and come back: they're not doing you any favours, just trying to make you feel better. If your ex seriously does think they've made a mistake, they'll call you themselves. Don't believe it unless the words come out of *their* mouth.

On the subject of friends, remember they have lives too. Make sure they know how much you've appreciated their support and put up with you knocking on their door at 3 am and phoning 65 million times an hour. It's okay if your conversations are still largely dominated by your break-up, but make an effort to spend even a quarter of it asking about them. As for striking up a friendship with your ex, it's too soon. Leave it a few months or longer to put some distance between you.

With seven days under your belt, it's time to organize and make sense of the thoughts and theories about the split that are whizzing around in your brain. If you have a good friend whose judgement you trust implicitly, ask them to help you diagnose the break-up so you can learn from the experience. Was it just bad timing and incompatibility or are you constantly falling for people who are bad for you? Do you grab onto anyone because you're scared of being on your own? Encourage them to be brutally honest and take whatever they say on the chin: if they know you well, there's at least a grain of truth in their theories. If you have a history of bad relationships, consider seeing a counsellor for a few sessions. At the very least, think about why you keep getting kicked in the teeth.

Feel especially tempted to call your ex after all this analysis? Don't! If you really must pour out all your intimate revelations (and are they really any of their business?), write a letter and wait two weeks before posting it. Chances are, you'll decide they don't need to know after all.

Week three

Okay, you cried when you found his old T-shirt at the bottom of the laundry basket or an old lipstick of hers under the bin in the bathroom. But you may find sadness being replaced by anger – white-hot, good-job-you-don't-own-a-gun type of anger. By all means, fantasize about taking revenge, but don't do it. Instead, get rid of the anger in a constructive way. A girlfriend of mine started running. 'I was so angry, I didn't know what to do with it so I started pounding the pavement.' She now has the best legs in London. Join a gym, take on extra work, get stuck into the garden: just do *something*!

By now, a certain amount of logic should be creeping in. Even if they came back, could you trust them not to leave you again? Even if you did call and beg for another chance, wouldn't you always wonder if they did it just because they felt sorry for you? Your brain's exhausted from diagnosing and dissecting the break-up and quite frankly, you're a bit sick of thinking about it. You stop taking all the blame for the split and realize it's rarely, if ever, one person's fault. Your friends stop worrying you're about to jump off a bridge and call less. Their eyes start to glaze over when you mention your ex's name. By week three, you're forced to spend nights alone and you feel okay about it. Not great, just okay. You still feel an overwhelming sense of loneliness and still wonder (for the 600th time) what they're doing at that moment, but it shouldn't be the focus of your existence. If it is, again, get yourself along to see a counsellor.

Week four

Life goes on. You're surviving without them, your heart is mending but this makes you feel despondent rather than satisfied. True love? Yeah, right. Forced to watch a soppy film, you scoff at the romantic bits and your friends accuse you of being cynical. You are – but that's normal. We all lose faith for a little while. If you're feeling depressed and unmotivated, take a good look at your health. You've probably been eating little and grabbing takeaways when you do. Resolve to eat healthily, cut back on the alcohol and ciggies and get a solid eight hours' sleep a night. The better you feel physically, the better you'll be able to cope emotionally.

If you find you can't stop thinking about your ex, try some aversion therapy. Put an elastic band around your wrist and flick it each time you think about them. You'll literally snap yourself out of it because it *hurts*. Your brain will start to associate thoughts of your ex with physical pain and subconsciously stop you thinking about them. When you flick the elastic band, say to yourself, 'I don't need you. I have my own life. I'm over you.'

The next month

Take a long look at yourself in the mirror. Are you happy with your appearance, your image and your wardrobe? The sort of person you are? If not, do something about it. Indulge in a personal trainer, get a friend with great dress sense to help you shop for new clothes, treat yourself to a course of massages and let a professional get rid of the tension of the last few weeks. Work on areas you'd like to change.

Start being a better friend, work harder, take some evening courses. Get back in touch with your sexual side as well. Start masturbating again, if you've stopped. Once your libido kicks back in, you'll find yourself checking out others in the gym (on the street, in your office) even if your heart and brain aren't interested in following through.

I still wouldn't suggest you hit the local nightclubs but you are ready for a restaurant, café, bar or pub. You're not out there to meet anyone, just for the experience of going out single. Don't take it personally if no-one checks you out, chats you up or appears even remotely interested. You're still exuding 'poor me!' vibes, even if you don't realize it. Your self-esteem should be climbing back up, but don't test it. Asking out the new-and-most-lusted-after person in the office isn't a good idea. You'll take it as a rejection even if they turn out to be married with six kids.

By the end of the month, you begin to feel remotely normal. The word's out that you're single and everyone's inviting you to this party or that dinner. Your diary is nicely packed full of dates and you've got things to look forward to. You feel rightfully proud of yourself for having coped and think you're well and truly over them until – a song comes on the radio and suddenly it all comes flooding back. You're laughing with friends and *she* walks past – only it's not her at all, just some girl with the same haircut. You go to dinner with friends and your eyes slide down their bookcase and see a travel book on Bali and a memory of the two of you poring over that holiday brochure hits you smack between the eyes. It hurts *intensely* and you think, *Oh God, I'm kidding myself. I'm not better at all.* But you are because the pain does *fade* – even if you feel faded from the experience.

It's most unfair but you'll probably find all

the memories of the two of you are good ones. Blame your brain. We idealize past relationships because our brains are programmed to throw up pleasant memories rather than painful ones. It's an instinct which usually works in our favour (to keep us as happy as possible) – but not in this case. Beat it by consciously dragging up a really unhappy, unpleasant memory about the two of you every time your brain throws up a good one. It puts things into perspective and helps ease the pain. Don't panic too much if you're still having the odd dreamy daydream about your ex months and months later. It's natural to think fondly of your last lover if you're a bit lonely single.

Two months later

You're laughing again. You're noticing things – like that great shirt or dress in the shop window (and the cute assistant standing at the counter). Life feels full of possibilities and after all those weeks of mooning around, you desperately want to *get on with it.*

It's around now that you suddenly feel the urge to meet someone new IMMEDIATELY! You still miss your ex but wonder if it's more the relationship you miss, than the person. By all means get out there and flirt your bottom off but do yourself (and them) a favour and keep any relationship you have on a casual basis for now. Give yourself time to grieve and heal and sort through all the baggage. The right time to start a fresh, new, serious relationship is when you honestly believe you understand what went wrong the last time and – even more importantly – feel confident of your judgement to pick someone who really will be good for you. Even then, take it slowly and keep both eyes *wide* open. Not just to protect yourself, but to see the new love of your life. Because if there's one advantage to breaking up, it's this: you get to go through that delicious falling-in-love stage, all over again!

LOVE BITES . . .

Q: How do you tell if your new relationship is headed for happiness or disaster?
A: Ask your flatmate. Researchers asked one member of a dating couple, one of their parents and their flatmate if they thought the couple would last. Six months and one year later, flatmates proved uncannily cluey at getting it right. The least correct? The couples themselves.

They're reckless, ruthless and unreliable. Constantly late, they check their reflection in the mirror frequently, interrupt while others are speaking, leave the lights blazing when they walk out of a room, run up debts, play hurtful practical jokes and aren't kind to animals. Who are they? According to US sociologists, this is a portrait of people most likely to cheat on their partners. After interviewing 107 couples, they discovered infidelity wasn't the only thing straying partners had in common. They also shared these key personality traits.

❗ Men carry the scars of divorce long after the relationship collapses – and it's all their wife's fault. Most men blame their wives not just for the problems which caused the split, but for the divorce as well (they did it because 'that was what *she* wanted').

❗ What's your fighting style?
  • The scream and sulk: 37 per cent of us rant then completely ignore our partner.
• The name callers: 28 per cent ignore

whatever it is they're arguing about and trade insults instead.
- *The talk and walk:* 25 per cent have shouting matches – which end when one of you walks out.
- *The long bicker:* Only one-tenth of couples surveyed bickered for hours and hours after the event – but at least *they* ended up solving whatever was bothering them in the first place!

Do you hate your ex with a passion or count him as one of your best friends? Surprisingly, neither matters when it comes to your ability to get over the break-up: it's how often you think about them that's the key. Intense but infrequent bursts of hatred are better for you emotionally than constant, cosy daydreams and trips down memory lane.

HOT RELATIONSHIPS
How to have one
by Tracey Cox

'Do not even attempt to fall in love or stay in love without this book' *Cosmopolitan*

Are you madly in love or driven mad by it? Happily single or looking for a partner? Living together, married with kids or dumped and desperate? Whatever the state of your love life, HOT RELATIONSHIPS has the answers to all your dating and relating dilemmas.

Funny, practical and refreshingly realistic, it's packed with advice on everything from flirting and flings to monogamy and marriage. There are hot tips on getting over an ex, where to meet a partner, how to spot the losers and how to breeze through that first date, as well as hints on fixing the fights, surviving jealousy and infidelity and breaking bad love habits.

A must-have manual for singles, couples, men and women, HOT RELATIONSHIPS shows you how to have one – and how to keep it that way.

From the author of the international bestseller *HOT SEX*.

0 552 14784 2

HOT SEX: HOW TO DO IT
POCKET EDITION
by Tracey Cox

'Frank, forthright and at times hysterically funny'
Cosmopolitan

Now you can have fantastic sex wherever you go with the
Hot Sex pocket edition. It serves up all the juiciest bits in a
handy take anywhere size. It's practical, explicit and fun,
with hundreds of steamy tips which will have you shredding
the sheets and begging for more:

- The famous 10-step guide to giving him a hellishly good
  blow-job
- Ohmigod-don't-ever-stop oral sex for her
- The hot new way to have intercourse (guaranteed to up
  her orgasm quota)
- His and her how-to-find-it guides to your G-spots
- Sex toys tried and tested
- Enough foreplay ideas to keep you amused for days,
  weeks, months . . .

Tracey Cox is one of the world's foremost (and hottest)
writers on sex and relationships, and is also a TV presenter.
Her numerous appearances include *Hotter Sex, Would Like
to Meet* as well as regular spots on the *Lorraine show*.

0 552 14956 X